screencraft

screenwriting

Declan McGrath
Felim MacDermott

screencraft

screenwriting

RotoVision

A RotoVision Book

Published and distributed by RotoVision SA

Route Suisse 9

CH-1295 Mies

Switzerland

RotoVision SA, Sales & Production Office

Sheridan House, 112/116A Western Road

Hove, East Sussex BN3 1DD, UK

Tel: +44 (0)1273 72 72 68

Fax: +44 (0)1273 72 72 69

E-mail: sales@rotovision.com

www.rotovision.com

ISBN 2-88046-363-7

10 9 8 7 6 5 4 3 2 1

Design Copyright © 1998 Morla Design, Inc., San Francisco

Layout by Artmedia Press, London

Production and separation by ProVision Pte. Ltd., Singapore

Tel: +656 334 7720

Fax: +656 334 7721

contents

introduction

'The young man who opened the door for her – he was 34 but still had unlined skin and thick hair, he had always been thought younger than he was, but what had irritated him in his early twenties now delighted him, as he saw his old school friends married or bald and he could still comfortably date girls ten years younger than himself – was also killed, although he took nearly 20 seconds to stop existing. Some of the display case had removed one of his legs completely and mutilated his groin and pelvis. Glass from the door had smashed open his face, ripping off his nose, and penetrated his brain. His name was Martin O'Hare. He had been to school. He had read "Great Expectations" and he wanted to be an astronomer. He had been in love with people and people had been in love with him. He too had a story.'

From 'Eureka Street', by contemporary Irish writer Robert McLiam Wilson, which tells the story of paramilitary killings in his home town of Belfast.

Here we are in Los Angeles, one whole ocean and continental landmass away from our homes in Ireland, introducing ourselves to celebrated screenwriter Robert Towne. Something about the glint in his eye suggests that we are going to enjoy this interview. "Hello Robert, my name is Felim," one of us begins. For readers unfamiliar with this Irish name the correct pronunciation is Fae-lum. If you are a Felim you can appreciate the significance of getting this right. Robert responds, "Felim... as in Felim Brady, the Bard of Armagh?" Perfect pronunciation. We were amazed.

'Felim Brady' is an old Irish ballad, one of many that helped record and shape our own culture and history. The ballad brings the listener into the mind of an old bard who recited poems and stories for noblemen. Reminiscing, he is devoid of bitterness or sadness for his lost youth, when he was the most enchanting young man in Armagh. Rather, he relishes the richness of his long life. We can recount the ballad because when we told Robert we had never heard it, he swiftly left the room, and began searching his house for the tape. When the song was eventually played, and as Robert's study steadily became smokier from his chunky cigars, he urged us to listen to a particular line: 'Merry-hearted boys make the best of old men'. "Isn't that a great line?" Towne reflected, punctuating his thoughts perfectly with a puff of his cigar. Something began to crystallise around this moment, something pointing to what is so very special about this collection of interviews.

While researching the art of screenwriting, we read many books about how to craft the perfect script. They all prescribe rules the authors have constructed and claim that by following these rules you will write a script that sells. Each book presents persuasive arguments as to why their particular system works. While reading these books, part of us sighed. There must be more to creating a screenplay than simply a collection of rules.

Of course there is more. There is individualism, and through working on this book we have had the honour of meeting and interviewing some of the greatest individuals in the history of screenwriting. But there is more to individuals than individualism; there is history, culture and tradition. The revelation for us has been the extent to which all of these factors have also informed the stories that the screenwriters in this book have been driven to tell.

If you listen, quietly and intently, to the heart beating in the scripts of these writers, you will hear stories born of a particular time and place, a particular set of experiences and view of the world. For example, in a work such as Krzysztof Kieslowski and Krzysztof Piesiewicz's **Dekalog**, we believe that you will hear a country whose humanity, morality and longing for the spiritual has been created by the devastation

of the Second World War and the brutality of totalitarianism. Hundreds of years ago, someone wrote the line, 'Merry-hearted boys make the best of old men'. That line still means something to people around the globe. The ballad recounts the life of an old bard, yet by listening to the heart of the ballad it also tells us about a country. By sharing such stories we can gain an appreciation of each other's culture.

At one time in Ireland, the ballad form was a means to preserve and tell stories. From the earliest days of community, bards and *seanachies* (storytellers) travelled around homes and villages and people would gather by flickering fires to hear them, enthralled by their tales of excitement and morality. The very same happened in other societies throughout the world. Nowadays cinema is the main means by which we tell our stories to one another. The screenwriter has the world as a potential audience and a multitude of aural and visual effects at their disposal. Yet the screenwriter's fundamental role is essentially the same as that of the oral storyteller. The baton of storytelling was passed on to screenwriters, as the inheritors of the oral tradition, at the beginning of the 20th century. In the early days of cinema, some audiences found the changing succession of images in the new films rather confusing. So in Japan, for example, when a film was projected, a *benshi* (narrator) would stand at the side and explain to the audience what was happening on the screen. The good *benshi* would learn from every performance what embellishments pleased an audience and next time changed the delivery accordingly. A similar person stood by the screen in African countries when cinema first arrived there. In Spain a man called the *mostrador* even had a long pointer to pick out characters as he explained the story.

As these preservers of the oral tradition became redundant, screenwriters began to appear. Early scripts took into account how the new medium might confuse an audience. Plot and characterisation were unambiguously clear and easy to follow. Actors physically expressed their emotions. The audience could be in no doubt as to what was happening on screen. Almost 100 years later, storytelling in cinema has become more sophisticated. Characters' motivations may not be so clear – the audience often needs to 'read' between lines of dialogue to work out what is happening. Dialogue may even be completely discarded, leaving a silence that can seemingly allow a confidential whisper of communication between film-maker and audience. Shades of hidden meaning leak out of the colours on the screen. Even the traditional idea of stories having a beginning followed by a middle and then an end can be challenged. Scripts go backwards and forwards in time, perhaps following several characters. These are all facets of a continuing and exciting process where screenwriters have changed and developed the way in which they tell us their stories.

The difficulties of screenwriting as a career have not changed so much from those early silent movie days. Thomas Edison ran one of the first film production companies. When Edison realised that he needed scripts, he sponsored a scriptwriting contest directed at colleges across America. The contest was not deemed a great success, as although 337 scenarios were submitted, only eight were judged to be of a good enough quality to be produced. Unfortunately for writers, this began a pattern that has continued to this day – the number of scripts written hugely outnumbers those that are made into films. An unrealised script is, by and large, worthless. A screenplay must find an audience. To reach that audience, it must be read and liked by financiers who are prepared to invest production finance into the script. Very few scripts get this production money. Next a producer will hire a director, cameraman, production designer, actors and many more crew to turn the script into a film. During the realisation of a script it will be altered by the approach of the director, the casting, choice of locations, lighting, costume and a host of other variables – the screenwriter's work will be constantly altered. When the film is finally made, all drafts of the script then become redundant. Only the finished film matters and the written word that created it is eclipsed – even a successful script is transitory.

Despite this fate, people continue to write for the screen, perhaps because however much a crew and circumstance may alter it, a script provides the story and theme of a film. The story is effectively the backbone of a film and the theme (where it exists) is its soul. When all else is stripped away, a film's fundamental essence, that which the audience reacts to, comes from the script. Writers will also continue to write scripts because cinema at its best can find an intimacy unavailable to the theatre and can communicate reality and sensation in a way not available to novelists. Most importantly, film, and its carrier TV, is the means whereby a writer can affect and influence more people than through any other medium.

The power of film in our modern world is immense. The 20th century was the era during which sound and pictures were used for propaganda as well as for creating stories and entertainment. Country states quickly realised the power of film, and so they imposed censorship. Of those featured in this book, George Axelrod, Robert Towne, Krzysztof

Piesiewicz, Jim Sheridan and Suso D'Amico have all had to contend with state interference in their writing. TV and film are today ostensibly subject to less controls. However, for a script to get funding it must be liked by one of a very small number of studio executives worldwide. Most of these executives work for large America-based multinational companies. These corporations have a myriad of other commercial interests and are motivated by profit. The common danger is that they will pick the scripts that sell a consumerist lifestyle and culture, with all its attendant products, as this is in keeping with their own interests, rather than those that tell stories representing the true variety of humanity.

These big multinational corporations not only choose the scripts to be financed but they control the methods of distribution. Their movies dominate cinemas throughout the world, leaving little space for a country's own indigenous stories. There is even less space again for stories from other countries. This means, for example, that there are less and less French films shown outside France, and more that is foreign (i.e. from the US) in France. As a result, there is less opportunity to see and hear films that allow us to learn about peoples and culture outside of America, as one kind of story and one view of the world appears to dominate our cinemas.

This is the grim reality of the marketplace in which screenwriters are trying to get their stories told. Screenwriters today are writing for the MTV generation, an impatient audience with a waning attention span; a generation suckled on promos made for an audience who watch without seeing and hear without listening, and whose own lives are faster and more fragmented than ever. In this modern world many believe that the whole idea of stories is under threat. They argue that we no longer need them. They say we now experience emotions and get an insight into humanity through the cyberworld of TV reality shows and internet chatrooms.

We disagree. Despite our fragmented and atomised world, we believe the demand for stories will remain as strong as ever. We will continue to need them to make sense of our own existence. We will also need them because they give us sheer pleasure, and the chance to break from the worries of the world by allowing us to experience the dangers of another world for two hours, while remaining in the comfort of our own seats. Basically, we need stories for the same reasons as people needed them during the time of Felim Brady, the Bard of Armagh…

The power of cinema gives the writer a great opportunity, but with that he or she also carries a huge responsibility. Great screenwriters who write from a deeply held passion and give us true stories rooted in experience, like the 13 featured in this book, help us to understand the life of others, whatever their culture and background. This is vital. When we realise that each person's life is a story, we realise how valuable each other person's life is. After the century we have just left, filled with world wars, totalitarianism, the Holocaust, civil strife and nuclear destruction, we wonder what could be more valuable than telling each other our stories, gathered around the global flickering light of cinema – just as our ancestors gathered around the campfire listening to their bards.

The authors would like to thank the following: Michael Bradley, Gavin Buckley, Mary Casey, Gerry Colgan, Marina Hughes, Anthony Kaluarachchi, Brian Kelly, Anthony Litton,

Patrick McGilligan, Andrew Melia, Anna Maria O'Flanagan, Ian Palmer, Adam Rynne, Robert Taylor, Joanne Kelly, Mairead McIvor, Nora Ephron, Pat and Rosie O'Leary, Peggy Owers, Mary Sherlock, Malgorzata Marcinkowska, Don Taylor, Galway Film Centre, Cork Film Centre, Larry Greenburg, Helen O'Dowd, Pat McGilligan, John Bailey, Mick Hannigan, Tomasz Korzeniowski, Jonathon Levine, Paddy O'Connor, Anna O'Sullivan, Bonnie Waitzkin, Shantalla movie club, Randy Haberkamp, Siobháin Burke, John Waggaman, David Murphy, Anne O'Leary, Laurie and Kay MacDermott, Michael Piers, Bruce Naughton, Ken and Joan Tuohy, Gerry Kelly, Brian Guickian and the McGrath Family.

Special thanks goes to our editor, Erica ffrench and the production controller Gary French, designers Andrea Bettella and Francesca Wisniewska, our transcriber Judith Burns, and The Ronald Grant Archive for the kind use of their pictures.

biography

Paul Schrader was born in 1946 in Grand Rapids, Michigan, where he received a strict Dutch Calvinist upbringing. Worldly amusements such as going to the cinema were prohibited by synodical decree. As a child he sneaked into town to see **The Absent-Minded Professor** (Robert Stevenson, 1961) and wondered what all the fuss was about. A year later he went with his cousins to see **Wild in the**

paul schrader

Country (Philip Dunne, 1962) with Elvis Presley, and he found out. At 17 Schrader went to Calvin College, Michigan, part college and part seminary, with the idea of becoming a minister. There he ran a film club and began to write about films. This interest led to him taking three short film courses at Columbia University, New York, during the summer of 1967. While at Columbia he was introduced to the film critic Pauline Kael who, impressed by his writings, encouraged him to attend film school at UCLA. There he edited his own magazine, *Cinema*, and was later film critic of the *Los Angeles Free Press*. Schrader has written four screenplays for Martin Scorsese: **Taxi Driver** (1976), **Raging Bull** (1980), **The Last Temptation of Christ** (1988) and **Bringing Out the Dead** (2000). He has also written and directed **Blue Collar** (1978), **American Gigolo** (1980), **Affliction** (1997) and the Japanese co-production **Mishima: A Life in Four Chapters** (1985). He is author of the book 'Transcendental Style in Film: Ozu, Bresson, Dreyer'. Schrader sees himself as part of a generation of screenwriters who always write "on spec" rather than being commissioned by studios.

Interview originally presented on 29 November 2001 as The Marvin Borowsky Lecture on Screenwriting for the Academy of Motion Picture Arts and Sciences recurring lecture series

interview

Art works. Art is functional, and artifice is a functional device to expose and illuminate one's own problems and put them in perspective and learn more about yourself and others. Art is as functional as a tool belt. It is not a plaything. It is not a diversion. It is not something you do when you don't have anything better to do. It is work, and the work of art is the work of any craftsman. If art works, and if that art can expose and organise and understand and put problems in perspective, then you the reader are the raw material, because we are the stuff of art. Screenplays are not about other movies, they are about people. Writers should not study cinema, they must study themselves. For first-time writers this can even be commercially beneficial, because when you are studying yourself, you are studying the only absolutely original thing that you know. Every other story is a copy. And why are they going to hire a first-time writer to do a copy of a teen exploitation film or an action film when they have got stables of perfectly talented, and thoroughly corrupt ego-deprived people who will actually do what they want, when they want and on the schedule they want? Why would they bother with someone who has no credits? If you are a first-time writer the only thing you have to offer is the fact that you are you. There must be something in your life that is unique and has some value. The writer must look at themselves, and when you write about yourself, of course, you are not only saying how you are different, but more importantly, you are saying how you are the same. Because in the end the way we are the same is more fascinating than the way we are different.

To be a writer you should first examine and confront your most pressing personal problems. We are in the dirty laundry business. The arts are about the forbidden, the untold, the unspoken and often the unspeakable. If you have a problem with pulling out your dirty laundry and passing it around, you are in the wrong business. Believe me, whatever hidden, hideous secret you think you have is not so surprising, and it is shared by a lot of people. When you find your problem, then come up with a metaphor for it. A metaphor is something that stands in the place of the problem. It is not like the problem. It is another variation of the problem. Where this first came to me was with **Taxi Driver**; the problem was loneliness. The metaphor was the taxicab. That steel, gaudy coffin floating through the sewers of New York, an iron box with a man inside who looked like he was in the middle of society, but in fact he was completely alone. The metaphor of the cab is so powerful that it can be repeated as a metaphor for loneliness. There was a speech early in the film where the taxi driver talked about loneliness, and Scorsese and I realised after the first screening that we could cut that speech out – the cab itself was doing the work. If you look at the great art, whether "Moby Dick" or "Frankenstein", you get a rock-solid metaphor. If it is really solid, it is more important than the plot, because there are only variations of plot. I think metaphor is harder to find. Once you

know it you will always know where the story started. This is important because as you write a script, you get very confused with plot and subplot and characters. When you come across a weak scene that is going nowhere, you'll ask yourself, what is the driving power of this whole story? That is why it is good to know the metaphor. Sometimes the metaphor will occur to you first and you have to back up and figure out the problem underneath that is making this metaphor appealing. Sometimes the problem comes to you before you have the metaphor. In **American Gigolo**, the problem was the inability to express love. I was teaching a course at UCLA at that time and we were going around the class and I said, "So what does this man do? Is he a salesman? Is he a businessman? Is he a carpenter? Is he a gigolo?" And right there, I said, "Wow, the inability to express love – the gigolo. That's it. That's the metaphor". Because here is a man who is in the business of providing love, therefore he is the perfect metaphor for someone who cannot express it. It is the representation of a thing by its opposite.

On **Light Sleeper** I wanted to do a mid-life movie and I tried to find a problem for years. I went through all the clichés: the fella who leaves his wife and takes off with a girl or goes off travelling. It was all so predictable and so boring. Then one night I was having a dream and this drug dealer that I knew appeared right in front of me. I woke up. It was about four in the morning and I said, "Wow, you know, I haven't seen that guy in five years. Why is he right there?" I realised I had been looking for him for a year and I could not find him. So finally he got tired of me looking for him and he came and looked me up. He was my mid-life protagonist. The drug dealer – the most vilified character in the culture. His mid-life crisis is my mid-life crisis. I started making notes right

RAGING BULL

CUM. PGS.	PGS.	
7 1½	1½	1. INTRO: JAKE SHADOW-BOXING IN TUX, DOING NIGHT CLUB MONOLOGUE
73 4	2½	2. REEVES FIGHT (1941)
86 7	3	3. JAKE-IDA-PETE: JAKE'S APT
89 10	3	4. JAKE TRAINS: GLEASON'S
11 12	2	5. NEIGHBORHOOD POOL #1: SEES VIKKI
13 14	2	6. ARMY PHYS
16 17	3	7. JAKE HITS IDA
	1½	8. NEIGHBORHOOD POOL #2
	1	9. JAKE + VIKKI: Mini-golf
22 21	1½	10. JAKE'S "RAPES" VIKKI
23	⑩	10A. SUGAR RAY'S PRESS CONFERENCE
24 23	2	11. GLEASON'S: prep for 3rd ROB
21 25½	2½	12. NIGHT BEFORE 3RD ROB
29 28½	3	13. 3RD ROB. FIGHT (1945)
33 31½	3	14. PETE GETS OUT
39 37½	6	15. CHESTER PALACE
40 39	1½	16. EMERGENCY WARD
95 41	4	17. MILO'S YONKERS HOME
46 43	2	18. WEIGH-IN FOR JANIRO
49 45	2	19. JANIRO FIGHT (1947)
51 44	4	20. SALVY SETS PETE UP W/VIKKI
54 52½	3½	21. DEBONAIR SOCIAL CLUB
	1	22. SALVY + JAKE
	1	23. JAKE + VIKKI
57	2½	24. DRESS SHOP: Jake beats up Pete
58½	1½	25. JAKE + VIKKI WATCH SUGAR ON TV
61	2½	26. FOX FIGHT (1947)
62½	1½	27. IDA + REPORTERS
65½	3	28. JAKE + JOEY
67	1½	29. PRE-CERDAN

(1) Rough scene outline from **Raging Bull**. (2–3) The young Schrader at the typewriter. "My life and my taste as a critic I regard as being a different fork in the road from my work as an imaginer of stories. Criticism and storytelling are two very different things. A critic is like a medical examiner. He opens up the body and tries to figure out how it lived and died. A writer is like a pregnant woman. He is trying to keep this thing alive until it is delivered. You must not let the medical examiner into the delivery room. He will kill that baby. So when writing I separate that critical part of my mind, because it just wants to keep me from embarrassing myself."

2

3

4

"From any book, there are a number of adaptations that can be made. There were about 12 different stories in The Last Temptation of Christ (1–4). In most books there are only two or three different stories. You have to find the story that means the most to you, that way you can write it with the same juice that the author wrote it with. Then find the author's intent. Hopefully you can then find a middle ground where those two meet."

then and there. That evening I had hooked up with him and three weeks later I had the script. The movie had been going on for 18 months, and all it needed was the metaphor. The drug dealer was it. Your metaphor must be different from the problem. If you are going to have any friction, if you are going to have any light, those two wires can never touch. There has to be some space in between them which allows you to jump.

Once you have settled on a metaphor, you move onto the next step: the rudiments of plot. We are not even talking about writing yet, but plot is the third most important thing. So ram the problem into the metaphor and see how the plot splinters out. What happens? Things happen. You learn about the true nature of the problem by exploring your plot. In the case of **Taxi Driver** I had assumed that the story was about loneliness. It is a very, very simple plot. He cannot have the girl he wants; he does not want the girl he can have. He tries to kill the father figure of one, fails; he kills the father figure of the other. That is the plot. But In working out that plot, you learn what the problem really was. The problem was not loneliness, it was self-imposed loneliness. The problem was the pathology of making yourself lonely. And that is where the healing part of art can come in because you realise that you are not really a lonely person, you are a person who wants to be lonely. Then you start to understand yourself.

The next step draws upon the oral tradition. I do not think that screenwriting is really about writing at all. I think it is about telling stories. Screenwriting has a lot more to do with the time your uncle went duck-hunting and the bird got away, than it has to do with great literature. You do not have to be particularly gifted in terms of craftsmanship of language to be a good screenwriter; all you have to do is be able to tell a good

story. If you can tell a story for 45 minutes, you have a movie. How do you know it works? Take anybody, preferably not someone who's too invested in either your ego or the so-called art of screenwriting, and say you want to have a drink and tell them the story. Tell it. Watch them. Watch their eyes. Watch their hands. Watch their ass! You know soon enough when you are losing them. And when you are losing them, work it and improve it. If you really want to be sure, after about a half-hour, go to the bathroom, come back and do not start the story up again and see whether they ask how it ends. Then you will know for sure whether you are telling a good story.

This telling of the story leads to the outline, which is just a list of the events in the story you have been telling. Scene one, man at podium, person stands up, leaves. Scene two, driving home alone, creates a mood. Scene three, gets home, there is nobody home. Where is his wife? Scene four, he gets on the phone. When you get enough "scenes" you can tell somebody the story again. The first time you tell the story it may be only 20 minutes long, but as you tell it, more things occur to you. Raymond Chandler once said that whenever you get in trouble have someone with a gun walk in the room – the reader will be so happy he is there that they won't ask where he came from. So, if you are telling your story and you are losing your listener, you say a red sports car pulls up and these two guys dressed in black get out. Bam. You got the listener back. You also got a red sports car with two guys in black. Now you have got to figure out what to do with them. As soon as you have finished telling it, you go back and jot down all the changes you made and then tell it again.

There is nothing more debilitating than writing scripts that do not get made or do not get sold. If you can put yourself

1

2

3

4

5

(1–3) Robert De Niro as Travis Bickle in **Taxi Driver**. The description of Travis Bickle at the beginning of the **Taxi Driver** screenplay: 'TRAVIS BICKLE, age 26, lean, hard, the consummate loner. On the surface he appears good-looking, even handsome; he has a quiet steady look and a disarming smile which flashes from nowhere, lighting up his whole face. But behind that smile, around his dark eyes, in his gaunt cheeks, one can see the ominous stains caused by a life of private fear, emptiness and loneliness. He seems to have wandered in from a land where it is always cold, a country where the inhabitants seldom speak. The head moves, the expression changes, but the eyes remain ever-fixed, unblinking, piercing empty space. Travis is now drifting in and out of the New York City night life, a dark shadow among darker shadows. Not noticed, no reason to be noticed, Travis is one with his surroundings. He wears rider jeans, cowboy boots, a plaid western shirt and a worn beige Army jacket with a patch reading, "King Kong Company 1968–70". He has the smell of sex about him: sick sex, repressed sex, lonely sex, but sex nonetheless. He is a raw male force, driving forward; toward what, one cannot tell. Then one looks closer and sees the inevitable. The clock spring cannot be wound continually tighter. As the earth moves toward the sun, Travis Bickle moves toward violence.'

"There is a kind of character that I have circled around. It is a person, usually male, who drifts around and peeps into other people's lives. He does not quite have a life himself and wants to have one but cannot figure out how to get it. I have always liked this character and obviously it was me. I was a kid from a strict Calvinist background who had seen 20 films in his life, all of a sudden thrown into LA in 1968 with people wearing tablecloths for dresses. I felt like a stranger and I had all this anger built up from my background. That conflict became the template for the character of Travis Bickle (1–3), and subsequently I have used him and modulated him over the years. So when he's 20 he's angry. He's lonely. He's a taxi driver. When he's 30 he's narcissistic and a gigolo [Richard Gere in **American Gigolo**] (4). When he's 40 he's anxious and a drug dealer [Willem Dafoe in **Light Sleeper**] (5). Hopefully, I will put that character to rest. It just gets too hard to finance these existential stories."

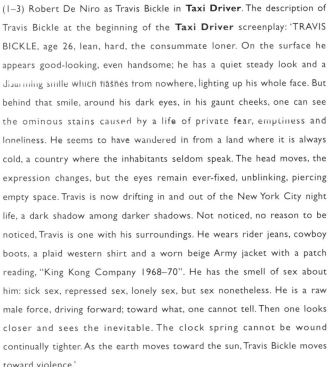

CHARLIE T cocks his imaginary gun again, fires and chuckles.
WIZARD and TRAVIS nod goodbye, pay the CASHIER and exit.

TRAVIS follows WIZARD out onto the sidewalk. TRAVIS follows
WIZARD as he walks toward his cab. He has something on his
mind, something he wants to talk to WIZARD about.

                    TRAVIS
               (walking)
          Hey Wiz.

                    WIZARD
          Yeah?

WIZARD leans back against the cab. TRAVIS is about to speak
when he spots a GROUP of BLACK and PUERTO RICAN STREET PUNKS,
ages 12-15, jiving down the sidewalk toward him. ONE tosses a
spray paint can around his back, basketball style. ANOTHER
mocks as if he's going to scratch a key along one of the
cabs.

WIZARD has no visible reaction. A flash of controlled anger
crosses TRAVIS' face. He stares at the BOY with the poised
key. It is the same look that crossed his face in the Harlem
Deli. We are reminded with a jolt that the killer lies just
beneath TRAVIS' surface.

The BLACK PUNK must instinctively realize this too, because
he makes a cocky show of putting the key back into his pocket
and be-bopping around TRAVIS and WIZARD.

The young mean-streeters continue down the street and TRAVIS
turns back to WIZARD.

Across the street, in the background, a JUNKIE nestles in a
doorway.

                    TRAVIS
               (hesitant)
          Wiz?

                    WIZARD
          Yeah?

                    TRAVIS
          Look, ah, we never talked much, you
          and me...

                    WIZARD
          Yeah?

                    TRAVIS
          I wanted to ask you something, on
          account you've been around so long.

                    WIZARD
          Shoot. They don't call me the
          Wizard for nothing.

                    TRAVIS
          Well, I just, you know...

                    WIZARD
          Things got ya down?

                    TRAVIS
          Real down.

                    WIZARD
          It happens.

                    TRAVIS
          Sometimes it gets so I just don't
          know what I'm gonna do. I get some
          real crazy ideas, you know? Just
          go out and do somethin'.

                    WIZARD
          The taxi life, you mean.

                    TRAVIS
          Yeah.

                    WIZARD
               (nods)
          I know.

                    TRAVIS
          Like do anything, you know.

                    WIZARD
          Travis, look, I dig it. Let me
          explain. You choose a certain way
          of life. You live it. It becomes
          what you are. I've been a hack 27
          years, the last ten at night. Still
          don't own my own cab. I guess
          that's the way I want it. You see,
          that must be what I am.

A police car stops across the street. TWO PATROLMEN get out
and roust the JUNKIE from his doorway.

                    WIZARD (CONT'D)
          Look, a person does a certain thing
          and that's all there is to it. It
          becomes what he is. Why fight it?
          What do you know?

1

4

2

5

                    WIZARD (CONT'D)
You're like a peg and you get
dropped into a slot and you got to
squirm and wiggle around a while
until you fit in.

                    TRAVIS
          (pause)
That's just about the dumbest thing
I ever heard, Wizard.

                    WIZARD
What do you expect, Bertrand
Russell? I've been a cabbie all my
life, what do I know?
          (a beat)
I don't even know what you're
talking about.

                    TRAVIS
Neither do I, I guess.

                    WIZARD
You fit in. It's lonely, it's
rough at first. But you fit in.
You got no choice.

                    TRAVIS
Yeah. Sorry, Wizard.

                    WIZARD
Don't worry, Killer. You'll be all
right.
          (a beat)
I seen enough to know.

                    TRAVIS
Thanks.

WIZARD gives TRAVIS a short wave implying, "Chin up, old
boy," and walks around to the driver's side of his cab.

WIZARD drives off, leaving the street to its natural
inhabitants.

A NEW FACE IN THE CROWD.

EXT. CHARLES PALATINE RALLY. DAY

A rally platform in a supermarket parking lot somewhere in
Queens is draped in red, white and blue bunting.

A crowd of about five hundred people strong mills about,
waiting for the rally to begin. Piped pop-country music plays
over the loudspeaker system.

3

6

7

(1–7) "This is a wonderfully unlinear scene

from **Taxi Driver**. It pops all over the place. It

is about people not connecting."

1

(1–4) "You use all kinds of layers in creating a character, including ones that nobody will spot. **Affliction** is about a cop, Wade Whitehouse, who had a very brutal father and who thinks there is a murderer in town. It turns out he was wrong. But there was a murderer. I said to Nick Nolte (the director), 'Wade is right, but the person who was murdered was Wade Whitehouse. But he is too hurt and too injured to realise that he was the victim.' Maybe one person out of a thousand will get that. But that is something we know and we can use in our own subtext."

2

3

4

through as many tests and hurdles as possible to get yourself to the position where you realise a script does not want to be written, you are doing yourself an enormous favour. Better to spend six weeks agonising over an idea and say "nope" and walk away, than six months writing it and then say it does not work. Try to figure out before you put one word to paper whether this idea really wants to be written. How do you do that? You outline it. You tell it. You retell it. You re-outline it. You live with it, and at some point the idea will either start to flag on you and bore you, or it will start to grow in intensity and it will start saying to you, "Get to the typewriter, it's time to go". And once an idea wants to be written, it happens fast. An idea that really wants to be written, will be written in 10, 20 days, that is all it takes if the idea is ready to go. When a student says, "Would you read this script? It's not much, I wrote it in two weeks", boy, my ears perk up. When somebody says to me, "I've been working on this for a year", I go, "Oh my God", because an idea should really want to be written.

I use the outlining method not only as a way to remember the story and tell it orally, but also as a way to pace it. To do this you have a list of all the scenes and have a projected page count running beside it. For example man speaks at podium, one page. Drives home, a quarter of a page. If you do that outline with some honesty, you will know what is going to happen on page 35. You will also know what is going to happen on page 76. In a way, you're pre-writing your entire script. You are not learning how to write it by writing it; you're learning how to write it by telling it orally. Of course, when you write it, it will change. That is the good news. However, if you have done your outline and you have planned that your protagonist finds out that the killer really is his stepbrother on page 65, and here you are on page 85 and he finds out, you

have made a mistake – either in your outline or in your writing. You have to decide which; if your mistake was in your outline, then you sit down and re-outline it to accommodate what you have learned by writing. If your mistake was in your writing, then you go back and try to figure out how to get 20 pages out of there. This may seem like the most uncreative way to write, but, at times, it has worked.

From the outline you finally write the first page of the script. Exposition, of course, is the bane of every writer's existence – you need to find a way to get exposition in there without being so naked about it. You have to explain the plot through dialogue. Remember that dialogue is often about people not connecting; as Harold Pinter said, language is the tool we use to not communicate. First-time writers write in such a predictable, linear fashion, not the way people talk, not the way people think. When you read a first-time script backwards it suddenly gets much more interesting, because the people are answering the questions before they hear the questions, which is what, in fact, happens a lot in life.

That is how I approach writing. I think every writer, if they are honest, admits that they taught themselves how to write. Writers read and then they figure out how to write. You cannot be prescriptive and say this is how you write a script and these are the secrets. There are no secrets. You can just tell what has worked for you. Perhaps the whole business of motion pictures is on its last legs. Who knows? Who cares? Storytelling will still be here. I do not care if they stop making movies. It is just another tool. I will put the hammer down, reach for the screwdriver and find another medium to work in. It is not about this sacred thing called the cinema. To me it's all about storytelling and self-exploration.

George Axelrod was born in 1922 in the Cambridge Hotel, New York. His mother was the silent movie starlet, Betty Carpenter. He became determined to be a writer while at boarding school, after reading Ernest Hemingway's novel 'The Sun Also Rises'. "I read it in two sittings and it changed my life. I said to myself, 'My God, writing is about conversations. I could do this'." Following expulsion from high school,

george axelrod

Axelrod entered the theatre as a stage manager and then a child actor, before becoming successful at his writing. He began to sell radio scripts at the age of 20, but his writing career was interrupted by three years of military service during the Second World War. When he returned to New York in 1945, he wrote comedy sketches for radio and began to work for TV. He also published the novel 'Beggars Choice' in 1947. Throughout this time he continued to write plays, completing 'The Seven Year Itch' in 1952, which became a massive hit on Broadway, as did his play 'Will Success Spoil Rock Hunter?' Axelrod wrote his first screenplay, 'Phffft', for Hollywood in 1954. He adapted 'The Seven Year Itch' for the big screen (Billy Wilder, 1955). It starred Marilyn Monroe, as did his adaptation of 'Bus Stop' (Joshua Logan, 1956). He earned an Oscar nomination for his script of Truman Capote's book 'Breakfast at Tiffany's' (Blake Edwards, 1961), before taking a new direction with the Cold War thriller, **The Manchurian Candidate** (John Frankenheimer, 1962). He continued to write scripts until the late '80s.

interview

During the '50s I had a big career as a playwright, with seven shows on Broadway. One night I was sitting at home in New York in my relatively cheap apartment, and the phone rang. The voice on the other end said, "This is Billy Wilder from California. The first thing you must do is get on the plane tomorrow and come to Hollywood because I need you out here very, very much and I cannot afford to mess around". I was in total awe of Billy and longed to work with him, and so I started as a scriptwriter. My experience up until then may have been writing theatre, but almost automatically I knew how to write a movie; and I'm not talking about writing "Scene 93, exterior, Mary's place". Anyone can do that.

In those days, Hollywood writers were the lowest of the low. "He's only a writer", they would say. Eventually Hollywood began to hire (non-screen) writers, that sort of changed things, but on the social scale the producers and directors were actually king. The writer was almost worse than the stunt guy! Personally, I can't complain because writing allowed me to live a certain way, and not have to go to an office – although

                    PAUL
                 (reading)
          Forget me, beautiful child, and may
          God be with you. Jose."

                    HOLLY
                 (after a moment)
          Well?

                    PAUL
          In a way it seems quite honest…..
          touching even…

                    HOLLY
          Touching? That square-ball jazz!

                    PAUL
          After all, he says he's a coward…

                    HOLLY
          All right, so he's not really a
          super-rat… or even a regular
          rat…he's just a scared little
          mouse.. but oh, gee, golly, damn...

She jams her fist into her mouth and begins to cry.

                    PAUL
          Well, so much for South America. I
          never really thought you were cut
          out to be the Queen of the Pamas
          anyhow.
                 (to driver)
          Croyden Hotel.

                    HOLLY
                 (to driver)
          Idlewood! (to Paul) The plane
          leaves at twelve and on it I plan o
          be…

                    PAUL
          Holly, you can't…

                    HOLLY
          Et pourquoi pas? I'm not hot-
          footing it after Jose, if that's
          what you think. No, as far as I'm
          concerned he's the future President
          of Nowhere. It's only, why should I
          waste a perfectly good plane
          ticket? Besides, I've never been to
          Brazil…

Holly reaches for her suitcase, opens it and takes out a
dress.

1

                    HOLLY (CONT'D)
          Please, darling, don't sit there
          looking at me like that. I'm going
          and that's all there is to it.
          Really you know, I haven't much
          choice…and what do I have to lose…
          except for the nickels put up for
          bail… bless O.J.'s heart…anyway,
          once on the coast I helped him win
          more than ten thousand in one poker
          hand. So I figure we're square…

As she talks she is pulling her sweatshirt over her head.

                    HOLLY(CONT'D)
          Now all they want from me are my
          services as a state's witness
          against Sally. Nobody has any
          intention of prosecuting me…to
          begin with they haven't a ghost of
          a chance…But even so…

She pulls the dress on over her head, then removes the blue
jeans under it. Then she finds a pair of shoes and the
dressing operation is now complete.

                    HOLLY (CONT'D)
          …this town's finished for me. At
          least for a while. They'll have the
          rope up at every saloon in town…I
          tell you what you do, darling…when
          you get back to town I want you to
          call The New York Times…or whoever
          you call…and mail me a list of the
          fifty richest men in Brazil. The
          fifty richest …regardless of race,
          color or present matrimonial
          status…

She suddenly becomes aware of the Cat who has climbed onto
her lap. She looks quickly out the window to see where they
are. The car is moving through a street in Spanish Harlem.

                    HOLLY (CONT'D)
                 (to the chauffeur)
          Stop here!

                    PAUL
          What are you doing?

Holly ignores him. The car pulls up to the curb. Holly opens
the door and, carrying the Cat, steps out.

2

EXT. HARLEM STREET - (DAY)

We find ourselves in a savage, garish neighborhood, garlanded
with poster portraits of movie stars and Madonnas. The
sidewalk are littered with fruit-rind and rotted newspaper
are hurled about by the wind. Holly stands for a moment
holding the Cat. She scratches his head and talks softly to
him.

                    HOLLY
          What do you think? This ought to be
          the right kind of place for a tough
          guy like you. Garbage cans…rats
          galore…plenty of cat-bums to gang
          around with… (she drops the Cat to
          the sidewalk) So scram!

Paul gets out of the car.

                    PAUL
          Holly…

The Cat looks up at her questioningly.

                    HOLLY
                 (to the Cat) I said beat it!

The Cat rubs up against her leg.

                    HOLLY (CONT'D)
                 (Angrily pushing the cat with her
                 foot) I said take off!

She jumps back into the car. Paul stands watching.

                    HOLLY (CONT'D)
          All right then…you can take off
          too!

She starts to close the door. Paul catches it and holds it
open.

                    HOLLY (CONT'D)
          Let go of the door! I'll miss the
          plane! Come on, driver, let's go!

She jerks the door closed. Paul reaches into his pocket,
takes out the red plush Tiffany box and tosses it to her
throw the window.

                    PAUL
          Here…I've carried this thing around
          for months…I don't want it any
          more.

3

CLOSE SHOT - HOLLY - (DAY)

She opens the box and sits staring at the ring. The car
starts and pulls away.

EXT. STREET - (DAY)

Paul stands watching the departing car. The rain has stopped
now and patches of blue are beginning to show between the
clouds. At the corner and the limousine stops for a light.
Suddenly the door opens and Holly jumps out. She is running
back toward him across the wet sidewalk. In a moment they are
in each other's arms. Then she pulls away.

                    HOLLY
          Come on, darling, we've got to find
          Cat…

Together they dash up the block and into an alley in the
direction the Cat had gone.

                    HOLLY (CONT'D)
                 (Calling) You cat! Where are you?
          Cat! Cat! Cat!(to Paul) We have to
          find him…I thought we just met by
          the river one day…that we were both
          independent….but I was wrong…we do
          belong to each other. He was mine!
          Here Cat, Cat, Cat! Where have you?

Then they see him, sitting quietly on the top of a garbage
can. She runs to him and gathers him in her arms.

                    HOLLY (CONT'D)
                 (to Paul, after a moment) Oh
          darling… (But there are no words
          for it

                    PAUL
          That's okay.

They walk in silence for moment, Holly carrying the Cat.

                    HOLLY
                 (In a small voice) Darling?

                    PAUL
          Yeah?

                    HOLLY
          Do you think Sam would be a nice
          name for Cat?

As they continue to walk up the street -

                    FADE OUT.

4

5

6

7

8

9

(1–9) "In all honesty, the ending of **Breakfast at Tiffany's** was sentimentalised, but what mysteriously made it work was the rain. Rain softens the reality in a funny way and there is something romantic about two people making love in it. I've used rain a lot! You would be amazed at what it does in a movie. The device of the goddamned cat at the end was also kind of fake and tricky. The cat features throughout the film, but Holly [Audrey Hepburn] never gives it a name (just referring to it as 'Hey, Cat') until the end, which then becomes all very romantic. The audience loves this kind of running feature in a film. In scripts familiarity does not breed contempt, it always breeds comfort."

you have to watch yourself because it's a sloth-producing life! It's so easy to say, "I don't feel like writing a goddamned scene today. Let me sleep on it!" You have no boss, nobody saying, "Get your ass in here and write the goddamned thing", except yourself, and I'm never that stern with myself.

During this period, scriptwriters were subject to censorship from the Motion Picture Production Code, enforced through the Hayes Office. My war with them was perpetual. I would fight with them every day. There was also the Catholic Legion of Decency. The guy there would say, "Now George, wouldn't it be better if I get Monsignor Biddle to sit down and write the scene with you", and I'd say, "Thank you very much, very kind of you both, but I don't think we want to do that". I would purposely put terrible vile things in the script so that they would demand to cut them out. Then I would agree to cut three out so that I could keep a couple of things I wanted. It was a continuous war. They were obsessed with any sexual connotation, and this made writing almost impossible. It was like writing with your right hand tied behind your back, and as you wrote you ended up censoring yourself.

Writing "Bus Stop", I would say, "Wouldn't it be great if the uncouth cowboy Beau could go in there and screw Marilyn? And while he was screwing Marilyn he could recite the Gettysburg Address to show he's literate?" However, in the final script he breaks into the room and merely stands by the bed and recites the address – not as effective as him going, "Four score and seven years ago our forefathers brought forth on this continent a new nation" while screwing her – now that's a funny scene. But they wouldn't let me do it! The script of **The Seven Year Itch** was certainly ruined by censorship. The play is based on a guy screwing a lady while his wife is away on holiday. In the movie script he is not allowed to screw the lady. So, his guilt is all nonsense, yet the guilt is what makes the play work. All his fantasies, like imagining his wife shooting him when she discovers what happened, do not make any sense if he hasn't screwed the girl.

As well as having problems with the Hayes Office, "The Seven Year Itch" did not really work as a film script. The play felt more claustrophobic; Sherman's imagination soaring beyond the apartment. Opening the location up, as in the film, dissipated a lot of the tension. Basically, certain stories will just not work as movies. The trick of adaptation is finding the heart of the piece and then taking that heart out and placing it into the other medium. It is like discovering the genetic code of the novel or play and knowing how to reconstitute it while retaining its integrity. It's not easy. A screenplay is the hardest form there is. When someone reads a book, they can look back at what went before to work something out. Cinema is all in the continuous now, and as a scriptwriter, you're not allowed any mistakes as the audience will be very critical. You basically have ten minutes at the head of your script to grab the interest and gain the trust of an audience. They'll listen to anything for ten minutes; and if they like it they will stay with you as long as you keep to your premise.

When writing a script I follow my instinct. If I get bored, then the audience will get bored, if I'm not excited by what I'm writing, then the audience is not going to be excited. So I stop, and a couple of days later I try and discover what went wrong. Then I work out that some new character should enter the scene or whatever. A lot of it is intuitive and, I fear, not something that can be taught. You can teach grammar and you can teach writing clear sentences with a beginning and an

1

2

4

Breakfast at Tiffany's: "Holly Golightly was totally Truman Capote's invention (2–3). I didn't use any of his plot because there was no story at all in the book, but I didn't invent the character In **Breakfast at Tiffany's**, that ridiculous Mickey Rooney character (4) which Blake [Edwards, the director] insisted on having does not work. Each time he appeared I said 'Jesus, Blake, can't you see that it fucks the movie up?' He said, 'We need comedy in this, and Mickey's character's funny'. But Mickey's character is a) not funny in that film, b) he has nothing whatsoever to do with the goddamned story. I got Audrey to agree to re-shoot the last scene, which was the only scene that she's in with Rooney, so I could cut out all the Rooney stuff. However, Billy kept it in." (1) Axelrod with Audrey Hepburn on location for **Paris When it Sizzles**.

3

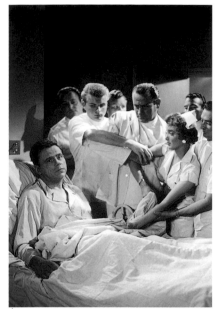

1

2

3

(1–3) "We like Richard Sherman [Tom Ewell] from **The Seven Year Itch** because he's scared shitless all the time and riddled with ridiculous guilt. His story is actually basically true. One summer when my wife and kids were away I was stuck in New York and did have such an affair with this most glorious girl. I felt so guilty about it that I thought I was going to die. Then I thought let's write about the guilt. I never wrote anything that wasn't based on the truth. Almost all my original material is based on a real person." (4–5) Draft changes to **The Seven Year Itch**.

2-1-2

Dr. Brubaker
This is therefore why my book is to be published with a cover depicting Gustav Meyerheim in the very act of attacking one of his victims....

Richard
I must take the responsibility for the cover myself, Doctor....

Dr. Brubaker
And also for making Meyerheim's victim -- all of whom, incidentally, were middle-aged women -- resembled in a number of basic characteristics, Miss Betty Grable?

Richard
I'm afraid so, Doctor. Don't you think there would be something just a little distasteful about a book jacket showing a man in the act to rape a middle aged lady?

Dr. Brubaker
And it is less distasteful of the lady is young and beautiful?

Richard
At least, if a man attacks a young and beautiful girl, it seems more...Oh my God. (He shudders)

Dr. Brubaker
I beg your pardon.

Richard
Nothing. Doctor, if you don't like the cover,I'll see if I can have it changed...

Dr. Brubaker
I would be much obliged.

Richard
Doctor.

Dr. Brubaker
Yes?

Richard
You say in the book that everyone in the world should be in need of some sort of psychiatric help.

Dr. Brubaker
This is theoretically true. It is not however practical. There is the matter of cost.

Richard
With your own patients -- are you very expensive.

Dr. Brubaker
Very. I demand and get fifty dollars an hour.

Richard
I'm sure you occasionally make exceptions—

4

2-1-3

Dr. Brubaker
Never.

Richard
I mean, once in a while a case must comes along that interests you...

Dr. Brubaker
at fifty dollars an hour all my cases interest me...

Richard
I mean if something really spectacular. You should run into Another Gustav Meyerheim for example...

(Dr. Brubaker just looks at him)

Dr. Brubaker
If Meyerheim desired my help it would cost him fifty dollars an hour.

Richard
Doctor. Tell me frankly. Do you think, just for example, that I need to be psychoanalysed?

Dr. Brubaker
Very possibly. I could recommend several very excellent men -- who might perhaps be a little cheaper. Seventy dollars an hour.

Richard
I couldn't even afford that...

How much cheaper?
Oh,...

Dr. Brubaker
I thought not. Now to get back to...

Richard
I wondered if possibly, you might give me some advice...

Dr. Brubaker
I know. Everyone wonders that.

Richard
I'm desperate doctor...Last night, after you left, I was just sitting here listening to the baseball game...

Dr. Brubaker
This fact in itself is not really sufficient cause to undertake analysis...

Richard
No, I don't mean that. I started out listening to the ball game. My wife and child are away for the summer you see --

Dr. Brubaker
Fifty dollars an hour... I have a young colleague...Dr. Samuals...

Richard
I don't know what came over me. I was listening to the ball game and do you know what I ended up doing...

Dr. Brubaker
(DR BEGINS TO gather his papers)

5

end, but you can't teach creative writing. I read voraciously to make up for my lack of formal education. If anyone is going to be a screenwriter they have got to read novels. Aspiring screenwriters must also go and see movies, and plays at the theatre, which are basic because of the three-act structure. Mainly, however, they've got to get off their butts and go in there and sit in front of the typewriter. You have got to actually do it because the only way to really learn how to do it is by doing it. Unfortunately!

In a way, you cannot directly learn from the great writers, rather they set examples which you feebly try to match. You wonder how did [F. Scott] Fitzgerald make the list of people that attended Gatsby's parties into such a brilliant four-page piece of literature? It's just a list of names, but it tells you all you need to know about Gatsby and the period. It's brilliant and magical. How wide does that tear your mind apart?

I never wrote a treatment in my life. I wrote an outline of what I felt the major scenes were going to be, and the order in which I felt they should be, but I never wrote a treatment. Each scene would be described in one line, numbered 1 to 20, say: (1) she comes to the house, (2) he does not know who she is, (3) we now discover in a flashback she has been sent there by the German police, and so on. Of course it ends up nothing like that, but I feel comforted to have this outline sitting there while I'm writing the script, because it means that there is some possibility that I'll finish it. If you write out a complete treatment, then I think you lose the energy that you need to put into the screenplay itself. It becomes a twice-told tale. I do have to know the beginning and the very ending to know where we're heading to, but the rest of it I love to leave open and see what magic happens (and I always regard it as magic)! Once I

get over the hurdle of looking at those blank pages, I generally like the writing part. I wouldn't have been a scriptwriter if it wasn't fun, because I found it extremely difficult to write if I wasn't enjoying myself in the process.

I've discovered there is one rule when writing comedy – it had better make you laugh! When I suddenly find myself laughing and writing at the same time I know we're home free. I think, Oh God, you've touched me, don't mess about with me, let me just keep going. I two-finger typewrite and I never learned to dictate successfully, because I lose something in doing that. I love the way words appear one at a time, a letter at a time, on a typewriter. I write what I feel in my head and I'm not even looking at the keys. Suddenly, at the end of a page I rip it out and I put another in. Sometimes I can do two or three pages of this. I only look at it a couple of days later, and oftentimes it's magical. Maybe it's the unconscious taking over. I don't know. Someone once told me that computers were great for writing. You can just press a button and change a character's name. As far as I'm concerned, you have got to go to court and throw out the script if you want to change a character's name! It is part of his identity. If I want to make a change I retype the whole page and each time it goes through the typewriter it gets tighter and better. You get the material to work by rewriting and rewriting. Once I have the structure right I do a final draft, and when we know who is going to play the characters the dialogue is polished so that it fits those particular actors. It's wonderful to write a script when you know who's going to play it – it reduces the number of possibilities. I had that with Audrey Hepburn on **Breakfast at Tiffany's** and on **Paris When it Sizzles**. **Bus Stop** was very particularly written for Marilyn Monroe. I could hear her voice. As you write the script, you know Audrey couldn't possibly say something so

1

2

3

4

(1–4) **The Seven Year Itch**: The image of Marilyn Monroe standing on top of the subway vent from **The Seven Year Itch** had been scripted by Axelrod (3). "We had to put a guy down there to make the wind blow through, and he just did it wrong and wrong and wrong, and I said, 'Come on, can't we get it right?' and he said, 'I just love looking up her dress!'" In the play, Sherman feels guilty because he has had illicit sex while his wife was absent. The Hayes Office would not allow Axelrod to include this in the film.

ROLL 122-1

ROLL 122-5

R 122-2

R 122-6

ROLL 122-9

R 122-3

R 122-7

R 122-10

R 122-4

R 122-8

R 122-11

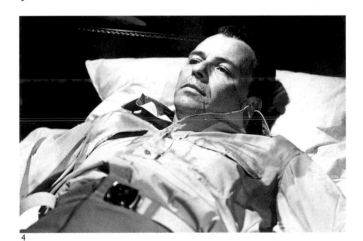

United Artists Corporation

729 SEVENTH AVE.
NEW YORK

VICE PRESIDENT

TELEPHONE CIRCLE 5-6000

February 26, 1963

Mr. Howard Koch
M. C. Productions
5451 Marathon
Hollywood 36, California

Dear Mr. Koch:

Re: MANCHURIAN CANDIDATE - Hong Kong

We have just been informed by our Manager in Hong Kong that
MANCHURIAN CANDIDATE has been irrevocably banned by the Censor authorities.

Although we lodged the strongest possible appeal the Censors
decision could not be reversed.

Kindest regards,

Sincerely,

Alfred Katz

/la

5

The Manchurian Candidate: "Raymond [Laurence Harvey], from **The Manchurian Candidate** was totally unsympathetic, which is very unusual for a lead. But he and his mother were both interesting characters (3). United Artists hated the whole goddamned thing. I wouldn't have got the picture made if we didn't manage to con Sinatra into doing it." Like George's sexual satires, **The Manchurian Candidate** also suffered from the censorship of the time (5). (1–2) Axelrod on the set of the film with lead Frank Sinatra.

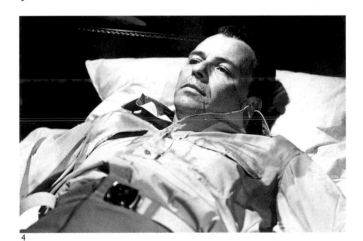

(1) Monroe with Billy Wilder and acting coach, and with Axelrod (3). "I always understood in some dumb instinctive way that Marilyn was very, very special and had to be handled in a special way. Nobody really knew how to handle her, but Billy did a little bit. She was an extraordinarily fragile creature, but the camera adored her. At one point I had a house just across from the back entrance of the Beverly Hills Hotel. One day I was having lunch with Marilyn on business and I said come on back and we'll talk some more. In order to get to my house you had to pass the back of the tennis courts, and she grabbed me and said, 'I always have to hold onto someone when I'm in spooky places'. Spooky places to her was the back of the Beverly Hills Hotel. She lived in continuous heartbreaking fear. It was very sad. In a proper world she should have been in a nuthouse." (2, 4) Stills from **Bus Stop**.

2

3

you just discard it, or that Marilyn couldn't possibly say it because it has two syllables! I knew Frank Sinatra (who starred in **The Manchurian Candidate**) well, and I understood his speech rhythms, so I knew how to keep it inside the area in which he was able to function at his best.

Work on **The Manchurian Candidate** started because I'd read a review of the book, and I thought it sounded interesting. It is about a patrol that is captured in Communist Korea, brainwashed and then sent back to sabotage the world. So I went across the street to a bookstore and I bought a couple of copies. After reading it, I called Frankenheimer [the director] and said, "John, come over and get this and read it". So he read it overnight and he said, "God we have to do this, but the only way I can get United Artists to buy this subversive piece of crap is to get a star attached". So we flew down to Miami where Sinatra was playing in a nightclub, gave him the book and, because I had known him a little bit from before, I said, "Francis, honour me by actually reading this son-of-a-bitch, will you? Actually you yourself, do not have somebody give you a synopsis, sit down and take an hour-and-a-half and read this thing. Do you promise?" And he swore and he did. And he called and said, "When do we start?"

People wonder whether the plot or the character drives the script. Supposedly the correct answer is that the character drives the plot and through that the script, but, come on, the plot drives everything and the character helps. The character is a piece of invention and it can't drive anything. I know I'm not in the majority, but that is my opinion. I admit there is a danger of inventing characters just to serve the plot, but because I have kind of an ear for dialogue, I can make the most implausible character sound reasonable for a certain

length of time. For dialogue, I listen to people and also as I write it I read the lines aloud to myself. In cinema you can't have as much talk as in theatre, therefore you make the material as visual as you possibly can. When I started scriptwriting, I found that I over-wrote dialogue, so it was a relief to cut out some of it and translate it into visuals. I learnt to do that rather quickly.

I always think movies drag on, so once the story is over, stick the words "The End" up there and get the hell out. One of the great faults in most drama forms is that everybody writes beyond the end. You get to the punch line and it's over, but instead the writer feels it's necessary to write three or four pages explaining what he did. I prefer to let the audience wonder a little bit. **The Seven Year Itch** resolves very quickly. All of a sudden, Sherman decides to leave Marilyn and he walks out the door and goes to see his family. The End. At the end of **Tiffany's**, as soon as the two finally kiss it's over. Truman Capote didn't like the ending; he thought I sentimentalised it by bringing the couple together and having them kiss. He felt it should end with the audience not knowing if the couple would get together. I don't know much, but I do know audiences don't like to be left to figure it out for themselves, you've got to tell them. So I put an ending on to structure it, which maybe was somewhat sentimental. Truman thought it compromised his work of art. It didn't. It made the movie a massive hit. What's the point of making movies that make people feel bad? When I go to the cinema, I don't go to feel bad, I go to have fun. Just as I always tried to have fun when writing. I also tried to make it the best I could do at that time. I never faked and I never hacked.

Steven Zaillian was born in Fresno, California, in 1953. Growing up, Zaillian was not really sure what he wanted to do, although he did think about following his father into journalism. It was only after attending a film studies course while studying at Sonoma State College, California, that he became interested in the idea of working in film. Following college he got a job as an editor with a B-movie production

steven zaillian

company. There he became friendly with some of the actors featured in the films. Together they began to see what film-making involved and felt that they themselves could make a movie. All they really needed was a script, and so Zaillian started writing. He had written two scripts before the third one, 'Bad Manners', was sold. A producer who was out-bid for 'Bad Manners' commissioned Zaillian to write another script, 'Alive'. Although not made into a film, 'Alive' came to the attention of director John Schlesinger, who then asked Zaillian to write the script for **The Falcon and the Snowman** (1984). This was Zaillian's first script to be made into a film. Since then he has gone on to write many other screenplays, including the Oscar-nominated **Awakenings** (Penny Marshall, 1990), the Oscar winner **Schindler's List** (Steven Spielberg, 1993), as well as contributing to **Clear and Present Danger** (Phillip Noyce, 1994) and **Gangs of New York** (Martin Scorsese, 2002). Zaillian has also both written and directed **Searching for Bobby Fischer** (1993) and **A Civil Action** (1998).

interview

The stories I write tend to be rooted in the real world. They are almost a combination of documentaries and theatrical films. My dad was a journalist, and the films that really spoke to me when I was at college were those that felt like real life, such as the neo-realist films and the French New Wave films. When I saw **Bicycle Thieves** and **The Four Hundred Blows** they had a huge influence on me.

It should not be unusual to be affected by films in this way, but it is and especially so today. The '60s and '70s were a good period for American films, but once the movie **Rocky** came out, everything changed in Hollywood. Suddenly movies had to be about a person succeeding and rising above adversity. They had to have a happy ending. Stories about real people struggling and maybe even failing became harder and harder to get made. When I try to sell a story about someone who succeeds through failure, the studio executives stare at me glassy-eyed, they do not know what I am talking about. But they are the stories that interest me – about people who, even though they are losing, continue to struggle on. To want to invest a year or more of my life writing a script, the story has to have some value.

The first thing I get hooked on is a feeling or a tone, sometimes an idea. Ultimately I think a script is about an idea – the character serves the idea, the plot serves both the character and the idea. That idea could be both strange and familiar to me at the same time. **Schindler's List** was completely foreign to me in terms of the particulars of its story, but there was something very familiar about the ideas in it. I do need to feel that these ideas do not only reside in the past, but are something that I have some experience of, or at least people I know have some experience of.

The inspiration for **Searching for Bobby Fischer** came from a photograph. Producer Scott Rudin had given me a stack of articles, books and ideas that interested him. Buried in the stack was a little book written by a young boy's father. It was the photograph on the cover that really got my attention – it was of a kid studying a chess position on a board. He was only seven years old, yet he was so adult and intense. This prompted questions in my head. Why was this kid doing an adult job? What kind of pressure does that put on the kid? As often happens, I was drawn to a particular world, chess in this case, in which the story takes place, and to a strong character in that world. Each chapter describes a different part of the chess world. Washington Square is a chapter, chess in Russia is a chapter, competitive chess and scholastic chess are all chapters. The author had obviously done a lot of research, and certainly enough from which to write the script. However, I felt that I needed to see these things for myself, and I did my own research, and that had an impact upon the script. By hanging out in Washington Square I met people in the park who became characters in the story. I also attended national scholastic chess championships. One in Knoxville, Tennessee, was amazing. It took place in a gymnasium normally used for sporting events like basketball. The first 20 rows were roped off with what looked like police tape because parents could not be trusted to not signal to their kids. This inspired the scene in the film where the parents are physically removed from the playing field. A lot of times research is simply verifying something that I hope I have right. I can then feel confident that I got it right, or make an adjustment to get it right. Other times the research suggests something that I never could have imagined.

In the case of **Schindler's List**, I purposely did no research until after writing the first draft, because I had heard that other writers on that film had done an enormous amount of research and become overwhelmed by it. I was nervous of falling into a morass of information and not seeing clearly the story that had to be told. So I did it in reverse. I wrote the basic story first and only afterwards did I speak to survivors and visit Krakow. Another ten drafts were written before the film was shot, which gave me plenty of time to selectively research whatever I needed.

Before getting to the first draft, I work for two or three months making an outline of the story. This outline is not something that I could present to anybody. It comprises 3 x 5" cards with scene titles on them and countless legal pads filled with notes. I am trying to get an overview of the whole film. I need to know where the story is going and what the basic signposts are along the way. These signposts are the scenes which are essential to tell the story. On the cards I describe the key part of each scene, which could be a location, or a character, or a

(5) The cover of the book about Josh Waitzkin, a child chess genius, which inspired Zaillian to begin writing the screenplay for **Searching for Bobby Fischer**. Zaillian spent time collating material, such as this notebook kept by Waitzkin (3–4), to help build up a picture of the real boy's personality. (1–2) Max Pomerac playing the role of Josh Waitzkin in **Searching for Bobby Fischer**.

Outline.doc / Feb., 1991

Rough Outline / Searching for Bobby Fischer

PART I:

    Normal kid; Washington Square; learning the game;
    Josh is a boy full of life!

PART II:

    Pandolfini; lessons; friendship between them; things
    still good; childrens' competitions; other parents "not
    like us."

PART III:

    1st big loss; not invincible; must work to be good;
    the real world; happiness wrapped up in Josh's winning;
    stripping away of his innocence and interests; trying
    to turn him into Bobby Fischer; the nadir: hates
    chess but has nothing left.

PART IV:

    Reclaiming Josh; recapturing his youth; making him
    whole again; and preparing him for the Nationals in an
    unorthodox original way.

PART V:

    The Nationals.

screenwriting

I

4

NOTES-3.DOC

* + DONE

(Revisions for 2nd Draft)

* 1-2 # Better/establish Fred at work.   DONE / But maybe change montage from stadium to football stadium.

1-2 # Show Fred (and Bonnie) interacting with people in their world, apart from chess.

* 1 # Maybe change the location of the scene when Bonnie tells Fred that Josh played chess in the park, from the den to an awards dinner (Fred loses?) or some other work or social function. If it's kept in the den, at least show what his work consists of.

* 3 # Get in the lines about "How many ballplayers grow up knowing they risk their father's love every time to go up to the plate," and Fred's response right back, "All of them." This just before he goes to California, in a scene where Fred's comparing Josh's losing to a batting slump.

The Thompson Street Coffee Shop?

2 # What about Pandolfini's connection to Fischer? Maybe he gave up serious play after watching (or playing) Fischer at a young age — much like Josh falls to pieces when seeing Poe play — seeing the beauty of Fischer's game and knowing he'll never be that good, so why do it.

Get Bonnie out of "the doorway."

1 # Show Bonnie interacting with other moms.

* 1-2 # Pandolfini (or Vinnie) on the beauty of chess.

* # Maybe the "beauty of chess, the majesty when it's played well," in the NY Open scene when Pandolfini is comparing Josh to Fischer — or — in the Pizza restaurant-Pac Man scene. (Beauty, symmetry, mathematics, etc.)

2 Also, or Josh could talk about this in his words — to his little sister (in his tent?) or Pandolfini or Vinnie (in the scene when Pandolfini first comes to see him play?) — how it's beautiful when the pieces align in a certain way — a work of art — a romantic view of the game.

So — we should hear what the game is to both Josh and Pandolfini. Two different scenes or one with them together? (in an old chess shop?)

A scene where Josh is taken to see ancient ornate chessmen at an old shop — by Pandolfini (second "lesson" — or before tournament montage?)

2

* # Maybe show/state more about how Josh is a combination of his father and mother (and all fathers and mothers) — the nurturer and the competitor — and subtly raise the question. Which side of Josh is going to win out?

More between Bonnie and Josh in the scene after 1st big loss — or follow her into the master bedroom for a scene between her and Fred — about decency, and time with dad, etc. (instead of the scene that's there now between Fred and Pandolfini.

PG-13 — clean up the language. ⟩ maybe the scene of Vinnie telling guys to shut the fuck up. The guys are talking about drugs or girls

Maybe more frantic at the Nationals — the way Fred used to be — and Fred seeing this like in a mirror.

* # Pandolfini admitting somewhere — that Josh (has) reawakened in him a love of the beauty of the game he had lost long ago?

* # One thing that Josh likes (and says) about chess is that — unlike other games, dice games, etc. — he makes the pieces move, can move them anywhere he wants — the freedom and beauty of that. It's closer to art.

Remember Charlie's phone number not "looking good" moment.

* # Maybe Vinnie's sign says something about him being a famous grandmaster "Beat Tal in 1957" — or something.

The hierarchy of the past guys? Guys who come and stand next to "greatness" hoping something will rub off on them.

Vinnie (or Vinnie?) leaving the park when another great player or hustler moves in?

Maybe Josh admits the fear of losing the special times with his dad if he loses — to his mother. Or she tells this to Fred.

Bonnie telling Fred maybe in Open House scene — or later before L.A. trip that she know Josh better than Fred does, having spent much more time raising him.

Shorten NY Open?

* # At the end of the NY Open scene — Pandolfini should talk more about Josh and the beauty of his playing, not just the goal.

3

1

4

(1–4) **Searching for Bobby Fischer**: "In **Searching for Bobby Fischer** (as in **Schindler's List** with Amon Goeth's character) there is one character who does not change at all. The boy remains the same while everyone around him is forced to examine their own selves. That is unusual, because normally it is the main character who changes." (1) Rough outline for the screenplay. (2–3) Zaillian's revision notes for the second draft of the film.

43

steven zaillian

> SCHINDLER
> (impatient)
> What?

> STERN
> There's a machinist outside who'd
> like to thank you personally for
> giving him a job.

Schindler gives his accountant a long-suffering look.

> STERN
> He asks every day. It'll just take a
> minute. He's very grateful.

Schindler's silence says, Is this really necessary? Stern pretends
it's a tacit okay, goes to the door and pokes his head out.

> STERN
> Mr. Lowenstein?

An old man with one arm appears in the doorway and Schindler
glances to the ceiling, to heaven. As the man slowly makes his
way into the room, Schindler sees the bruises on his face. And
when he speaks, only half his mouth moves; the other half is
paralyzed.

> LOWENSTEIN
> I want to thank you, sir, for giving
> me the opportunity to work.

> SCHINDLER
> You're welcome, I'm sure you're doing
> a great job.

Schindler shakes the man's hand perfunctorily and tells Stern with
a look, Okay, that's enough, get him out of here.

> LOWENSTEIN
> The SS beat me up. They would have
> killed me, but I'm essential to the
> war effort, thanks to you.

> SCHINDLER
> That's great.

> LOWENSTEIN
> I work hard for you. I'll continue
> to work hard for you.

> SCHINDLER
> That's great, thanks.

(1–8) **Schindler's List**: "This scene is the first time that Schindler has to
confront any feelings for the Jews working in his factory. His clerk Stern
[Ben Kingsley] creates a situation in which Schindler is forced to put a face
on his workers. Stern hopes this will make Schindler start feeling
responsible for them. Schindler is basically saying to Stern, 'I do not want
to be that person, so do not do this to me'. In case the audience did not
get it, this point is made again in the scene following it. None of this is said
directly. Often in a scene you cannot listen to the words, you have to figure
out what characters are not saying, or which lie they are telling. In real life
people almost never tell the truth. The key moment in the first scene is the
line, 'You're a good man'. There has to be enough dialogue in order to
make the line feel natural and have it work."

> LOWENSTEIN
> God bless you, sir.

> SCHINDLER
> Yeah, okay.

> LOWENSTEIN
> You're a good man.

Schindler is _dying_, and telling Stern with his eyes, Get this
guy _out_ of here. Stern takes the man's arm.

> STERN
> Okay, Mr. Lowenstein.

> LOWENSTEIN
> He saved my life.

> STERN
> Yes, he did.

> LOWENSTEIN
> God bless him.

> STERN
> Yes.

They disappear out the door. Schindler sits down to his meal.
And tries to eat it.

73   EXT. FACTORY - LATER - DAY   73

Stern and Schindler emerge from the rear of the factory. The
limousine is waiting, the back door held open by a driver.
Climbing in -

> SCHINDLER
> Don't ever do that to me again.

> STERN
> Do what?

Stern knows what he means. And Schindler knows he knows.

> SCHINDLER
> Close the door.

The driver closes the door. Stern slowly smiles.

74   EXT. GHETTO GATE - DAY   74

Snow on the ground and more coming down. A hundred of Schindler's
workers marching past the ghetto gate under armed guard, showing
their identity cards with the holy Blauschein.

3

4

5

6

7

8

1

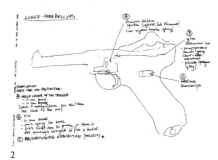

2

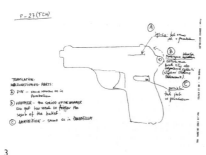

3

(1–5) **Schindler's List**: For Zaillian, research is an important part of the scriptwriter's job. He interviewed Holocaust survivor Poldek Pfefferberg to learn about the black market in Krakow in 1940 (4). In one scene in the film, the SS commander Amon Goeth [Ralph Fiennes] fails to kill a worker because his gun does not work (5). Zaillian spent time researching ways in which such a gun would not work (2–3).

+ The blackmarket (according to Pfefferberg)

    Forbidden, illegal. Jews were expected to live on
    their rations and not buy or sell anything.

    Everything was hard to get, you could triple the price.

    Dangerous because of informers.

    Because of his looks and attitude, Pfef could get away
    with it.

    Most dealings took place in private homes. Also on the
    street, but it was dangerous just to be seen talking to
    someone.

    St. Mary's Church. Dark. Sit and pray and deal. Guy
    like Pfefferberg goes in, deals with another Jew or
    with a Catholic.

    Once he exchanged a million zloty (in two suitcases)
    for occupation currency minus the 15% payoff to his
    friend at the Reich Bank that did it and his own
    commission.

    Most of the time people would sell stuff to buy food.

    No Jewish stores owned by Jews by 1940.

    Often times the goods would be bought and sold five
    times through middle men before reaching the actual
    buyer.

    A guy had a good wine cellar in the ghetto.
    Pfefferberg would sell to Schindler and others.

    The shoe polish deal: Pfef bought lots of shoe polish
    from a guy (in glass containers), sold it to a German
    who sold it to sold it to the Army - but, because of
    the cold, the glass broke; the guy blames Pfef who
    blames the guy who sold it to him, tells him he'll give
    his name if he doesn't replace it with metal
    containers. Done.

    Cotton wicks for gas lamps. Pfef buys a couple hundred
    yards of it from one German-run company and sells it to
    another German-run company; made a lot of money.

    Something about syrup (for scarce sugar).

4

SCHINDLER'S LIST   95.   FINAL DRAFT

                    GOETH
        That's very good. What I don't
        understand, though, is - you've been
        working since what, about six this
        morning? Yet such a small pile of
        hinges?

He understands perfectly. So does Levartov; he has just crafted
his own death in exactly 75 seconds. No one looks up from their
work as Goeth leads the rabbi past their benches and out the door.
He stands Levartov against a low wall, and adjusts his shoulders.
Behind the condemned man, workers pushing stone trolleys veer to
the edges of the angle of probable trajectory of stray bullets
before Goeth pulls out his pistol. He sets the barrel against
the rabbi's head and pulls the trigger - click.

                    GOETH
                (mumble)
        Christ -

Annoyed, Goeth extracts the bullet-magazine, slaps it back in and
aims at the ground. Click. Groaning to himself, he pulls out
another gun, puts its barrel against Levartov's head. He pulls
the trigger and the rabbi's head sways as if it could absorb the
impact of the bullet like a punch. But again there's only a
click.

                    GOETH
        God _damn_ it -

                    LEVARTOV
        Herr Commandant, I beg to report that
        my heap of hinges was so
        unsatisfactory because the machines
        were being recalibrated this
        morning - I was put on to shovelling
        coal.

He slams the weapon across Levartov's face and the rabbi slumps
dazed to the ground. Looking up into Goeth's face, he knows it's
not over. As Goeth walks away with his faulty guns -

171 EXT. PLASZOW - DAY   171

A gold lighter in Schindler's hand flames a cigarette.

                    SCHINDLER
        The guy can turn out a hinge in less
        than a minute? Why the long story?

He hands the gold lighter to Stern and walks away toward a D.E.F.
truck being loaded with supplies.

5

description of action or a line of dialogue. I will only write dialogue at this stage if it is the key part of the scene. All scenes have a "key part" or emphasis, and it may be at the beginning, the middle or the end. The rest is window dressing in order for that action to happen, those words to be spoken or that piece of music to come in.

Once I know those half a dozen "signpost scenes" and I have convinced myself that I know enough about the story, I will start. It's a delicate matter knowing when to start, as I think it's possible to know too much about a story. There should still be some discovery to be made during the writing. The actual writing normally goes quite quickly. I begin on page one; I do not skip scenes, and if a scene is not going well or I do not like it I will slug through it one way or another rather than jump ahead to another part of the story. Often it is something between those signpost scenes, where I have no idea in advance of how it is going to go, that really turns out nice.

I will often be the only one that reads the first draft. I will give the second draft to friends and people whose opinion I trust and admire. Finally, I will turn the third or fourth draft over to the studio when I feel that 90 per cent of the work has been done. If I get back 20 pages of notes from the studio, there is no reason to continue because I'm already 90 per cent happy with it. Most of their notes are about making the character or plot clear. I will usually try to explain that it is clear enough. The danger is if you make something too clear you're treating the audience like children. Inevitably there will be six to ten more drafts that need to be done, but they address small things rather than reconceive anything. Mostly it is editing. When you edit you take something out which you have to fix with something else, and that can be very time-consuming.

On **Schindler's List** I had originally written a very lean script. When I say lean, for me that is 130 pages – although for other people that is a long script. That first draft was solid in terms of telling the story. When Spielberg got involved, he encouraged me to put in things that he had heard about or that were in the book but were not necessary in order to tell the story. That was the first time that anybody had ever encouraged me to add scenes that were not specifically plot or character driven. If you have too many such scenes you will go off track and you may not be able to come back. But if they do not derail the story they can give you a fuller view, because you are examining events on the edges as opposed to right down the centre. You need to have a story that is quite streamlined and simple and knows where it is going before adding such off-subject scenes. **Schindler's List** may feel like a big story, but if you examine it, it is quite simply told. In order to get through all of the possible stories I made a rule for myself that there would be no scene that did not have something to do with Schindler. Even then it could still have spun out into an unmanageable narrative, so I had to focus on certain aspects of the story. I concentrated on telling the story of the Holocaust from a business standpoint. I followed the money, because that was the world that Schindler was in and that was what interested him.

My scripts are often longer than the average script because I try to imagine, for my own purposes, what is happening in each scene. For example, I mention what the person is thinking, and what they look like. Sometimes I go back and take those things out, because they are really more for me than for anybody else. Other times my descriptions are intended for the director. For instance if I write, "From this distance they were quite small against the horizon", the first

EXT. BRINNLITZ - DAY

All eleven hundred of them, a great moving crowd coming forward, crosses the land laying between the camp, behind them, and the town, in front of them.

Tight on the FACE of one of the MEN.

Tight on TYPEWRITER KEYS rapping his NAME.

Tight on A PEN scratching out the words, "METAL POLISHER" on a form.

Tight on the KEYS typing, "TEACHER."

Tight on his FACE in the crowd.

Tight on the face of a woman in the moving crowd. The keys typing her name. The pen scratching out "LATHE OPERATOR" The keys typing "PHYSICIAN." Tight on her face.

Tight on a man's face. His name. Pen scratching out "ELECTRICIAN." Keys typing "MUSICIAN." His face.

A woman's face. Name. Pen scratching out "MACHINIST." Keys typing "MERCHANT." Face.

The names and faces of everyone we recognize, and their professions before the war.

"CARPENTER." Face. "SECRETARY." Face. "DRAFTSMAN." Face. "PAINTER." Face. "JOURNALIST." Face. "NURSE." Face. "JUDGE." Face. Face. Face. Face.

                              HARD CUT TO:

EXT. FRANKFURT - DUSK

A street of apartment buildings in a working class neighborhood of the city.

From somewhere, like a memory, echo the distant, plaintive strains of "Gloomy Sunday."

Legend: Frankfurt, Germany, 1955

INT. APARTMENT - DUSK

A 78 of the melancholy Hungarian love song turns beneath the needle of a cheap hi-fi.

The door to the modest apartment opens and Oskar Schindler is revealed inside. The elegant clothes are gone but the familiar smile remains.

                    SCHINDLER
          Hey, how're you doing?

It's Poldek Pfefferberg out in the hall.

                    PFEFFERBERG
          Good. How's it going?

                    SCHINDLER
          Things are great, things are
          great.

Things don't look so great. Schindler isn't penniless, but he's not far from it, living alone in the one room behind him.

                    PFEFFERBERG
          What are you doing?

                    SCHINDLER
          I'm having a drink, come on in,
          we'll have a drink.

                    PFEFFERBERG
          I mean where have you been?
          Nobody's seen you around for a
          couple of weeks.

                    SCHINDLER
               (puzzled)
          I've been here. I guess I haven't
          been out.

                    PFEFFERBERG
          I thought maybe you'd like to come
          over, have some dinner, some of
          the people are coming over.

                    SCHINDLER
          Yeah? Yeah, that'd be nice, let
          me get my coat.

Pfefferberg waits out in the hall as Schindler disappears inside for a minute. The legend below appears:

          AMON GOETH WAS ARRESTED AGAIN,
          WHILE A PATIENT IN AN SANITARIUM
          AT BAD TOLZ.

          GIVING THE NATIONAL SOCIALIST
          SALUTE, HE WAS HANGED IN CRACOW
          FOR CRIMES AGAINST HUMANITY.

Schindler reappears wearing a coat, steps out into the hall, forgets something, turns around and goes back in.

          OSKAR SCHINDLER FAILED AT
          SEVERAL BUSINESSES, AND MARRIAGE,
          AFTER THE WAR.

          IN 1958, HE WAS DECLARED A
          RIGHTEOUS PERSON BY THE COUNCIL OF
          THE YAD VASHEM IN JERUSALEM, AND
          INVITED TO PLANT A TREE IN THE
          AVENUE OF THE RIGHTEOUS.

          IT GROWS THERE STILL.

He comes back out with a nice bottle of wine in his hand. He remembered that but forgot to turn the hi-fi off and "Gloomy Sunday" keeps playing as he and Pfefferberg disappear down the stairs together -

                    SCHINDLER'S VOICE
          Mila's good?

                    PFEFFERBERG'S VOICE:
          She's good.

                    SCHINDLER'S VOICE
          Kids are good? Let's stop at a
          store on the way so I can buy them
          something.

                    PFEFFERBERG'S VOICE
          They don't need anything. They
          just want to see you.

                    SCHINDLER'S VOICE
          Yeah, I know. I'd like to pick up
          something for them. It'll only
          take a minute.

Their voices fade. Against the empty hallway appears a faint trace of the image of the factory workers, through the wire, walking away from the Brinnlitz camp. And the legends:

          THERE ARE FEWER THAN FIVE
          THOUSAND JEWS LEFT ALIVE IN POLAND
          TODAY.

          THERE ARE MORE THAN SIX THOUSAND
          DESCENDANTS OF THE SCHINDLER
          JEWS.

                              FADE TO BLACK

UNDER END CREDITS:

Moving slowly over the road of fractured gravestones winding through Plaszow. Tuffs of grass and weeds between the spaces. A pick pries at one of the stones, and -

Thousands of mismatched fragments of unearthed stones on the ground like pieces of a jigsaw puzzle. A workman's hands place two together that fit, and -

A wall under construction, a memorial made entirely of the recovered gravestones. Moving across them, two letters of a name are all that remain of one, four letters of another, then a full name, then half a name, three letters of another, two, and, finally, only a Jewish star.

R E P O R T

on activity and expenditures for the rescue of
Jews during the years 1939 to 1945, by manager
Oskar Schindler, owner of the enamel factory at
Krakow, and its evacuated works "Working Camp"
Brünnlitz, Czechoslovakia.

Some days ago I have been approached officially by high Jewish personalities
who spoke to me about details of the rescue of 1100 Jews of my
store houses, to write down a comprehensive report about my activity to
give a global impression of my actions to outsiders and to exclude any
possible diminution of the facts from the very beginning.

When I came to Krakow in 1939, to build up my life-carreer in economics,
I rented, and later bought, an empty factory hall through the Polish
Commercial Court at Krakow (from the bankrupt's estate Rekord). There
I started with the production of enamel crockery. I did not consider the
possibility of managing one of the numerous factories and shops as trustee,
because I hated, from the very beginning, the Trust Agency with their
authorization to run Jewish property, and their way of handling business.
As lessee, and later owner, of the firm founded by me, I was my own boss,
independent of any authorities. The great demand of crockery brought my
business quickly to a boom, and, due to my efficiency, I was able to
enlarge my factory considerably. After three months I employed already
250 Polish workers and employees, among them 7 Jews. (1940 I had 150 Jews,
1941/190, 1942/550, 1943/900, 1944/1.000 and 1945 over 1.100 Jews .
With the persecution of Jews, which began in 1942 within the entire Polish
area, by excluding them from daily life, liquidation of gettos, and the
opening of annihilation camps, I was put before the decision to either
dispense with the collaboration of Jews, to leave them to their fate, as
99% of the Krakow's firms, who employed Jews, did, or to build up a private
storehouse of my own firm and to put them into barracks. My mental attitude
toward my Jewish workers helped me to overcome the threatening difficulties.

Within few days a storehouse was built, and hundreds of Jews saved from
compulsory transfer. I have also taken over Jews from neighbouring stores
of other firms, i.e. from the firm ... Neue Kühler- und Flugzeugteilefabrik
(New Radiator- and Aeroplane-spare parts factory) Kurt Hodermann at Krakow,
box factory Ernst Kümpast at Krakow, and barrack-works of the local
army administration (Heeresstandortverwaltung) Ing. Schailevski, and, in
doing so, saved 450 Jews from compulsory transfer. I can proudly maintain
that, only due to my initiative, these Jews could stay at my camp, because
all interventions and negotiations regarding the Jews, with SS authoritie
were handled by me intrepidesly. The creation of the factory's camp

5

could only be carried out with my private monies, without any support or
financial help authorities. To take care of the equipment was completely
left to the employer. It sufficed that security regulations demanded by
the SS, were complied with.

In the enclosure I will quote the large sums spent by me during the years,
from my private sources, to finance the rescue action of the "Schindler-Jews".

1. Dwelling Camp Krakow:
For this purpose I bought a piece of estate from Mr. and Mrs. Brilski.
It had to be established; Fencing, watch towers, numerous barracks,
canalization, baths, lavatories, doctors to be hired, a dentist's ambul-
atorium, laundry, hairdresser's room, food store, barrack's office, guard
block for guards, as well as furnishings for dwellings, kitchen and dentists.

2. Food Expenditures:

During the years 1942-1944 almost 100% of foodstuff requirements had to be
bought on the "black market", since Jews, with the exception of the so-
called "barracks-catering" of the concentration camp Krakow-Plaszow, which
amounted to hardly 40% of the nourishing minimum, did not receive any supplies
and of which I also made, secretely, considerable quantities available to
the concentration camp. During all these years I received only six to
eight times very small quantities of supplies from the JUS (Jewish Relief
Organization), i.e. parcels containing semolina destined for sick and juvenile
The monthly average of food requirements for my Krakow factory kitchen,
from black market source, is estimated with 50.000 Zloty as rather low.

3. Over-Occupation, Disabled:
Due to my giving in to my Jews requests to save also their disabled parents
and relatives from compulsory transfer, and to officially employ them in my
factory when allocated another 200 - 300 new "workers", I had difficulties
with such a great number of practically unusable people, because my production
on the long run, did not justify their employment. Approximately 200 Jews
can be considered as over-employed and disabled. To the cashier, of course,
(cashier of the SS and Police Leader) I had to pay per day and per person
5 Zloty, with the intention of appearing to SS authorities as a firm always
lacking workers.
4. Bribes and "Contributions":
I was forced to pay bribes to the party, and, as well as compulsory contributions to various collections like Red Cross, Winter-aid, musical west
Programs, etc., whether I liked it or not, to keep my firm running, which
* had already the reputation of being very amicable towards Jews, furthermore

6

7

(1–7) **Schindler's List**: Spielberg encouraged Zaillian to draw in scenes
that were not essential to the main thrust of the story. (1–4) The final
scene from an early draft of the screenplay. (5–6) Extract from Oskar
Schindler's account of events, which were subsequently chronicled in
Zaillian's screenplay. This research material helped Zaillian understand the
real Schindler's character.

1

2

3

(1) Still from **A Civil Action** and (2) Zaillian writing on the set of the film. (3) Photograph from the 1988 screenwriters' strike. "Unlike anybody else on a film, Hollywood writers are interchangeable, and when you start feeling like you are interchangeable you take a bit of offence. If directors were brought in one after the other until they found one that they liked, the Directors Guild would never allow that. When you sign an actor you are stuck with them and you get a performance as good as they give you. I think a lot of writers, myself included, feel that when you are hired as a writer you should be the only writer."

thing that comes to mind is certainly not a close-up. The director now "sees" the scene the same way I do, and I've not resorted to the awkward screen direction, "Wide Shot". Description is also a way of controlling pace. If you come out of a scene that has a lot of description to set a mood and you go into a scene that is pure dialogue like a play, the reader will speed up the pace of that scene in their mind. I will write a slower-paced scene slower, using more words in order to slow it down. The writing style changes in order to create an experience for the reader equivalent to watching the movie.

Both description and dialogue are integral parts of writing a scene. Sometimes dialogue is incidental and it is really the visual that is important. In **Searching for Bobby Fischer**, the mother and her son are walking down the street in one scene and the mother asks if he wants to go and get some pizza, and he replies, "I don't know, maybe, maybe not". This dialogue is totally incidental. The important thing is that he is looking ahead at Washington Square, because that is where he wants to go. While the dialogue in a scene like that is unimportant, you still have to have it. Other times I will write a scene where there is virtually no description of the setting, because what is being said is the only thing that matters.

When I am writing dialogue and I know that there is one line which is the important key moment, I still have to get there naturally. I need to decide how far back to go in the conversation before that key line. You often find out later that you only need two lines before that important one and it still feels natural. You may not need, "Hello, how are you doing, it's nice to see you again", but all that gets you into the scene. On a lot of scenes the front end of dialogue will later come off. You can normally cut off the first ten minutes of any film and

it would still make sense. The writer will often spend time introducing the characters before the plot starts. I think this is natural, because first-time writers do not know their characters and so they try to put them in situations to explore who they are. Every student film ever made starts with somebody in bed. An alarm clock goes off and they get up out of bed. The film-maker is trying to imagine the story right from the beginning and imagine how the character moves and talks and gets dressed in the morning. You can almost always cut that stuff out and start the movie in the middle of a plot. Start with the story rather than an introduction to the story.

The book of **Schindler's List** spends the first 50 pages telling you who Schindler was before he went to Krakow. It describes his boyhood, him growing up, being a young adult and marrying his wife. My script starts with him arriving at Krakow. I decided to get the important backstory into the film some other way, although I did not know how. The temptation is to tell the audience as much as you know yourself at the beginning of a story. Instead you should allow the audience to discover who the characters are and what it is that they are trying to achieve. There is a scene in **Schindler's List** where Schindler declares that his goal in Krakow is to make lots of money and go back rich and famous. The temptation is to put that scene first. It is probably at page 40 in my script, and it works much better there than if you put it earlier.

Certain stories have been told for thousands of years over and over and over again, and we need a steady diet of these stories. I do not think that you can be told such stories too much. Life is a constant struggle against one form of adversity or another. Maybe it is of some value to experience that in stories.

Jim Sheridan was born in 1949 and grew up in inner city Dublin. There he began acting with the St Lawrence O'Toole Players, that had been set up by his father following the death of one of Sheridan's brothers. At 21 he joined the acting school attached to Dublin's Abbey Theatre, leaving after some time to direct his own production of 'Dr Faustus'. A job as a TV announcer made Sheridan enough money to go to

jim sheridan

53

University College Dublin, where he continued his involvement in the theatre. After college he formed a street theatre company with a group that included the Irish actor Neil Jordan. From 1975 to 1981 he ran Dublin's Project Arts Centre where he would regularly run into conflict with the city's councillors over shows that challenged the sexual and political status quo of the city. In 1982 Sheridan left for New York, taking over the New York Irish Arts Center. His first feature film was **My Left Foot** (1989) which he both directed and wrote the screenplay for. This film began his working relationship with actor Daniel Day-Lewis, who has appeared in Sheridan's **In the Name of the Father** (1993) and **The Boxer** (1997). Sheridan has also written **The Field** (1990), **Into the West** (1992) and produced and co-written **Some Mother's Son** (1996).

When I first arrived in America and I asked New York cab drivers to bring me to 51st and 10, they would bring me to 54th and 10. In my Dublin accent "first" sounded like "fourth". I had to say 51 and 10 to be sure that they would bring me to the right street. I realised that in America, because it is an immigrant culture, everything has to be clear. Even having numbers rather than names on the roads helps make it clear. In America a transparent language has built up that allows people from different cultures and backgrounds to communicate clearly and directly with each other. This contrasts with Irish culture; there have been times when if you had communicated clearly you would have got killed. This is because I come from a culture which has been dominated and oppressed. So rather than direct communication we use sarcasm and irony; an American will accept "have a nice day" at face value whereas an Irish person will suspect that you are being sarcastic. Although the American way of transparent communication loses certain shades of irony that make life interesting, as a scriptwriter I prefer what you gain in terms of always being clear. I want to be like the Americans and be always clear to all cultures. I do not want to spend my life telling stories that do not connect. When I write, I am trying to communicate; art is what happens when communication is at a deep level.

The system the Americans have adopted to communicate clearly in cinema is the traditional three-act structure. I began to learn about structure after I left theatre and entered the world of film. In theatre the absurdist avant-garde destroyed structure as a reaction to the apparent absence of meaning in the world after the Nazi death camps and the atom bombs at Hiroshima and Nagasaki. Only in the populist entertainment of cinema was the traditional Ibsen three-act structure maintained. Ironically, the relatively new industry of cinema, supposed to be the most avant-garde, is actually very conservative in the way that it tells stories. Film is a time medium and the job of the writer is to create emotions which the audience respond to in a time structure.

People like Syd Fields [American screenwriting analyst] have examined this structure, showing how Hollywood movies tend to follow the traditional three acts. You start the first act by laying out the background to the story and establishing the main character. Ten minutes into the script, you have the inciting incident. This incident lights a "fuse" which will "blow up" in a scene towards the end of the first act, usually 30 minutes into the film. This scene will shatter the audience's perception of the film, and take the hero off in a new series of complicated directions. Throughout the second act the complications pile on top of the hero until at the end of that act, about 90 minutes in, he is in the worst situation possible and all looks lost. Then, in the third and final act the hero overcomes the difficulties and you resolve the plot

complications. Most Hollywood movies follow this structure. It works with audiences because they are used to the pattern and they feel safe with it. A general audience knows nothing about the inciting incident, but they are so used to it that if something does not happen ten minutes into the film then the story feels slow. However, although the rules are there to lay out what the public are accustomed to, people think they do not actually want to go and see what they are accustomed to. A writer must manipulate the story within the conventional structure while trying to make it seem unconventional and unexpected to the audience. The three-act structure helps writers by saying do not make every scene a masterpiece, make the turning point at the end of act one exciting and do the same with the scene at the end of act two. If the writer can then have a strong denouement scene, even better. When I write I plan the story to get to these big scenes where I will have everything worked out word for word. You cannot have the whole two hours made up of one scene better than another. Young writers try to write every scene as a work of genius. Even Shakespeare would always have lesser scenes, where maybe letters would arrive explaining elements of the plot.

When I started writing, it was for theatre, for small audiences and for little money. I tried to change the world. All I knew about stories was that they were supposed to have a point of view. Now in the movie business, I write scripts for the big sow that is Hollywood and try to milk it dry of money. I can do nothing else because film is a commercial business and without production money a script is worthless. Yet, even in this commercial world, I still do not see the purpose of writing unless you have a point of view. When I am writing sometimes that strong viewpoint means too much emotion pours onto the page and the story becomes too driven for an audience.

(1–8) The scriptwriter can create sequences of
parallel action, as here in **Some Mother's
Son**, where the overall effect of the combined
scenes is greater than the individual one.

EXT. SAFE HOUSE. DAY

Gerard approaches the side entrance. Frankie and IRA
MAN no.2 leave with a heavy bag.

INT. SCHOOL. CLASSROOM. DAY

Kathleen watches the girls practice their dance steps.

EXT. COUNTRY ROAD. DAY

Kathleen's car pulls up at a country lane. Frank,
Gerard and IRA MAN no. 2 get out. They go to the back,
take out the rocket launcher. Frank climbs over a gate
by a field, followed by IRA MAN no.2. Gerard keeps
watch.

INT. SCHOOL. CLASSROOM. DAY

The beat of the dance tune intencifies, the dancers'
feet pound the floor as…

                                    CUT TO:

EXT. GLENARM. BRIDGE. DAY

Frank and IRA MAN no.2 run toward a hedge.

Frank's P.O.V. through the rocket launcher sight: A
bridge, soldiers lay explosives.

INT. SCHOOL. CLASSROOM. DAY

The girl's dance, now in slow motion as:

EXT. HEDGE. DAY

Frank fires the launcher.

A loud band and a trail of smoke from the hedge.

INT. SCHOOL. CLASSROOM. DAY

Kathleen hears the roar of the rocket.

EXT. GLENARM. BRIDGE. DAY

The missile smashes into the jeep, an explosion,
followed by a larger explosion which consumes the jeep.

INT. SCHOOL. CLASSROOM. DAY

Windows shatter, girls cry, duck to the ground. Smoke
rises from across the field.

AAT. COUNTRY LANE. EXT. CAR. DAY

Frank and IRA MAN no.2 run back through the field.
Gerard waits nervously.

Frank and IRA MAN no.2 tumble into the car.

INT. SCHOOL. CLASSROOM. DAY

The girls flee the classroom. A young girl is
hysterical. Kathleen shelters the girl and leads her
out.

EXT. SCHOOL. DAY

The girls flee the school as bells sound and in the
distance sirens wail.

EXT. COUNTRY LANE. DAY

The car speeds away.

EXT. GLENARM. MAIN STREET. DAY

A street of white-washed cottages and small corner
grocery stores. Frightened women at doorways, young men
at corners, clearly excited, some elated.

```
EXT. NUMBER TEN DOWNING ST. DAY

Margaret Thatcher, newly elected, enters the building, speaks
to reporters (archival video footage).

                    THATCHER
          I know full well the
          responsibilities that await me as I
          enter the door of Number Ten, and
          I'll strive unceasingly to try to
          fulfil the trust and confidence
          that the British people have placed
          in me and all the things in which I
          believe. And I would just like to
          remember some words of Saint
          Francis of Assisi, which I think
          are particularly apt at this
          moment, "Where there is discord,
          may we bring harmony…"

                                        CUT TO:

EXT. SEA. DAY.

The Northern Ireland Coast. Dawn. A fishing boat sails into
an inlet. Gerard, 20ish, and Paddy, mid 40's, clean fish as
they sail back to Glenarm harbor.

                    THATCHER
          "Where there is error, may we bring
          truth. Where there is doubt, may we
          bring faith. And where there is
          despair, may we bring hope."

The boat pulls into the dock. Gerard and Paddy tie up the
boat. They unload fish. Paddy notices something across on the
cliff's edge.

                    PADDY
          What are those bastards doing at
          the bridge?

Gerard looks to see.

A British Army convoy is gathered on the top of the cliff at
a small bridge.

EXT. INLET HARBOUR. DAY

Gerard and Paddy continue unloading.

The Brits blow the bridge.

Gerard spins around
```

3

(1–9) **Some Mother's Son**: A scriptwriter can juxtapose and overlay sound and image to powerful effect, as in this opening scene from the film (3–9).

It is like being stuck in the pub with someone who is telling you a very personal story and you begin to feel that this person is compelled to tell you that story whether you want to hear it or not. You start to feel uncomfortable. Structure can help the writer avoid creating that uncomfortable feeling in the audience. It works as a necessary impediment to that potential torrent of emotion. So for people with passion and commitment (which should include the writer) the three-act structure may be something that helps fashion the turmoil of their inner lives into something explainable. Of course your script must communicate emotions. Because they are invisible, emotions are actually hard to write. Sometimes the most powerful part of a story is invisible. When I was a kid watching TV sometimes the reception would go. First the horizontal hold would go and then the vertical hold. The images would appear sideways or else they would run. Yet although I could not make out the visuals clearly, I could still follow the story. Even if I lost the pictures the engagement that I had in my head with the story and its emotions made it work. I became convinced that you did not need to see all the images all the time.

As you write you are aiming to manipulate the audience's analytical mind yet at the same time trying to build up emotional moments. If you succeed in creating such moments and the story works, the audience will be grabbed. Without making any effort they will move up onto that flat cinema screen and start identifying with some character, and become immensely involved in the life of that character. The viewer begins to feel that their own life depends on whether this character survives. At this point the story starts to play by itself in the audience's head and they begin to imagine their own world. For example many people describe the great battle scene in **Gone with the Wind**, but there is no battle scene, just its aftermath. The audience have gone into that flat cinema image and imagined their own totally real world 360 degrees around their head. When I was a kid, after seeing cowboy movies I used to run home for two miles because my energy was so fired up by the story. The writer wants the audience to leave the cinema with the film still playing in their heads and to go to a restaurant and talk about it. That happens when you have brought the audience up onto the screen. You achieve that by getting them to connect with a character on the screen. The writer cannot make the audience connect with the characters solely through dialogue. Watching a film is like being thrown into a jungle on a survival mode – the eyes are prominent and sound is second. The audience reads situations according to the facial expressions of the characters. It is almost like our first few months of existence, before we can speak, when life is basically a close-up of our mother's face. Emotions are mostly conveyed by looks and body language, words are a definite second. So when you are writing for cinema you have to get into a space where you can imagine what the character's facial reactions are going to be.

To create a story that the audience will accept it needs an emotional charge. That charge comes from the writer talking about a subject that means something to him. Most writers want something they have not got, perhaps the love of their father or their mother or their girlfriend. They often extract that emotion through writing. Great writing is usually when a writer discovers a moment of change in himself and then finds a vehicle through which he can dramatise that change. While writing **My Left Foot** I personally was changing from feeling like a victim, having worked in the theatre for no money, to feeling that I wanted to take control. The story of **My Left**

57

jim sheridan

Foot (about the emotional development of a disabled person) reflected this change. **The Boxer** probably contains too little change. It is too illustrative. It illustrates the character of a good guy who went to prison for fighting with the IRA but who now works to help rebuild his community. This brings him into conflict with those who still believe in violence. This character had no change to go through. The audience found it hard to identify with him because he had no weaknesses. You cannot write an illustrative drama, box it up and then sell it to the public. The only way is to fill it with explosions and special effects.

For me **The Boxer** actually was an emotionally charged story. Because of Irish history and Irish society, to say that you are against violence and support the vision of Catholics and Protestants working together (like the character in **The Boxer**) was actually something radical. The problem was that for the rest of the world and particularly America, being anti-violence was not new! So a theme could be emotionally charged for one country and yet seen as illustrative for the rest of the world. In Afghanistan, a film about a free woman would be very radical, but in America the reaction would be "so what?" A particular audience's reaction is strongly influenced by the society it lives in. At the same time that particular audience along with every other audience (the mass audience) reacts to the society you write about according to how it compares with the American model. This is because all audiences think they live in that American society. For example, in 1969 people in Northern Ireland marched for civil rights because they thought they had a Bill of Rights — something they had seen on American TV. Everybody in Ireland thought they were in America, and getting their heads battered did not convince them otherwise.

So the easiest thing to do is to make an American film. When you are writing about non-American values you have to explain them to the audience, and do so in a way that does not seem like you are explaining it to them. This may be hard to do, but if you succeed you have the extra benefit of the exotic which the audience will enjoy because they have not seen it before. **In the Name of the Father** starts with tanks chasing a guy down a city street. Then you see the father, a pacifist with a white handkerchief, enter the fray. These arresting opening images set up a messed-up society with values different from the American norm. American writers do have an advantage, in that they can set up their stories much more easily. It is similar to having a movie star because the audience already knows who that star is going to play and so the writer does not have to explain his character. The trick for non-American writers is to find out how your particular perspective relates to everyone else all over the planet.

When I was approached to write the story of what was known as the Guildford Four, four people who were wrongly imprisoned by the British, the first thing that struck me was that this was a family which was imprisoned. I knew that in America they would have been called the Conlon family or the Maguire family rather than the Guildford Four. Making it into a story about a father and son, a family story, internationalised it. Western society's development has been accelerated by TV and film, to a point that it has almost eclipsed religion. In countries where there is no TV, they are at the start of fundamentalist religion. The differences in the world are so great that it could lead to nuclear conflict.

Perhaps we should start thinking about such subjects rather than always about entertainment. At the moment when you

3

1

4

2

5

In 1972 British Army soldiers shot and killed 13 civil rights marchers in Derry (1–2). "The events of Bloody Sunday affected me very much. When I saw the innocent people getting killed I wanted to go out and get a gun. Instead I started writing. The oppressed person is often afraid or else not allowed to speak their mind. This inability to communicate becomes a cancer. It leads to violence because violence is communication on the lowest level. For me, communicating your anger and your blame is healthy. As a writer I examine myself and try to change myself, and then try to see if I can have a peripheral value to society by suggesting other ways. Exploring the injustices delivered by the English on the Irish gives me a charge." (3–5) "With **In the Name of the Father**, the story of Irish people who were wrongly imprisoned by the British, I used the three-act structure and the American system to make a story that the British TV networks would not touch. So I made this revolutionary story through money from a very conservative American institution – a film studio."

156 INT. WING. DAY.   156

All the prisoners watch a new man, Joe Mac Connell, descend
the stairs from th TWOSto the breakfast line. He gets his
food, turns heads towards the cockney tables. Gerry warns
him.

                    GERRY
          You can't go down there.

                    JOE MAC CONNELL
          I'll sit where I want.

Mac Connell walks on towards a table, cups are thrown at
him. Finally two cockney gangsters stand in his way. Mac
Connell throws his breakfast round one, loafs the other.
More cockneys pile on.

Guiseppe emerges from his cell, watches the commotion from
the TWOS ⎯⎯⎯

Gerry throws down his breakfast and runs to help Mac
Connell.

A wild fight.
Screw intervene, drag the bloody figures of Joe and Gerry
out the gate and off to Solitary.

157 INT. WING. DAY.   157

A screw shouts from the main gate of the ONES.

                    SCREW
          Two on.

Gerry and Joe, slightly bruised are led in to the wing and
up the stairs to the TWOS. Guiseppe waits. Joe and Gerry go
up to Guiseppe.

                    GERRY
          Da come on inside, I've something very
          important to tell you.

58   INT. CELL. DAY.

Guiseppe enters folowed by Gerry and Joe.   158
                    GUISEPPE
          What.

                                        (CONTINUED)

:. 5, april 5

---

158 CONTINUED:

                    JOE MAC CONNELL
          I'm the one who bombed Guildford, Mr.
          Conlon.

                    GERRY
          (excited) Joe says he'll do whatever
          he can to help us.

                    JOE MAC CONNELL
          I'm sorry you're in here, Mr Conlon ..

                    GUISEPPE
          (interrupts) don't be sorry for me, be
          sorry for the innocent people you
          killed.

                    JOE MAC CONNELL
          It was a military target_ a soldiers
          pub.

                    GUISEPPE
          They were God's children.

                    GERRY
          (shamed by Guiseppe's hostility) Da!

                    GUISEPPE
          I'd appreciate it if you left us
          alone.

                    JOE MAC CONNELL
          Whatever you say Mr. Conlon.

Mac Connell leaves.

                    GERRY
          What are you doing?

                    GUISEPPE
          I want no part of him or his ways.

                    GERRY
          Why, because he stands up for himself,
          because he's able to fight back,
          something you've never done.

                    GUISEPPE
          What do you mean?

                    GERRY
          Remember when you used to give me a
          ride on the crossbar of your bicycle,
          and one day you couldn't make it up
          the hill. I had to get down, in front
          of everybody. I walked in front of you
          and when I looked back your face was
          all red. It was the paint shed, wasn't it ?

screenwriting

1   2

4   5

(1–7) **In the Name of the Father**: Script excerpts and frames from a
key scene exploring the fraught relationship between Gerry (Daniel Day-
Lewis) and his father Giuseppe (Pete Postlethwaite).

"The actual drama of **In the Name of the Father** – arrest, conviction,
escape – is like any other prison story. Running parallel to this prison story
is the tale of how the good hard-edged pacifist father (8) dies and his son
(9) takes on his role. That is the theme. So below the structure, which
everyone can understand and see, there is the underlying thematic idea."

                GUISEPPE
        I don't know what you're talking
        about.

                GERRY
        It was breathing the fumes at the
        paint shed where you were sick not
        jumping off the boat to swim back to
        mammy.
        The only job a catholic could get, and
        still you wouldn't fight back.

                GUISEPPE
        (angry) Go on about your business with
        your new friend.

                GERRY
        You've been a victim all your life,
        it's time you started to fight back.

                GUISEPPE
        Get out of my sight!!!

159   INT. WING. DAY.

      Most of the prisoners file out for exercise. Mac Connell
      watches from the TWOS, sees Ronnie Smalls and a couple of
      his cronies sit at their table, reading papers chatting. Joe
      looks over towards Gerry, who sits on the landing having a
      smoke. Joe nods to Gerry to join him.
      They meets at the stairs to the Ones.

                JOE MAC CONNELL
        Come on.

      Gerry follows, slightly apprehensive. Joe followed by Gerry
      walk to Ronnie Smalls table. Joe pulls up a chair.

                RONNIE SMALLS
        What the fuck do you want, Paddy.

                JOE MAC CONNELL
        I was just wondering if you know where
        54 Halsey Road is?

                RONNIE SMALLS
        (slightly flustered) Yeah I know where
        it is.

                JOE MAC CONNELL
        (leans in to Ronnie) No offence
        Ronnie, I don't want to take anything
        away from you but this intimidation of
        us is going to stop, otherwise I'll
        have 54 Halsey Road blown up with your
        family in it.
        So let's be friends.

      Joe gets up, walks away with Gerry.

                        (CONTINUED)

      5, april 5

3

6   7

8   9

(1–5) **My Left Foot** tells the story of the severely disabled Christy Brown (Daniel Day-Lewis) who becomes a celebrated writer. "Empathy is crucial in a film. **My Left Foot** is told in flashback. The opening shot shows the adult Christy placing a needle on a record with his left foot and then staring defiantly at the camera. Then we show his childhood. If you started the film with an incapacitated baby the audience would want that child to walk by the end of the film. If you start the film with the character at 30 years of age and still only able to move his left foot the audience knows it is not a story about a physical disability. It is about a person with cerebral palsy but who is the same as you and me, because emotionally he is messed up."

5

write for cinema you can only go so far exploring such important themes without getting into real trouble in obtaining funding. Perhaps contemporary writers and film-makers should get inspired by the punk-rock revolution of the '70s. Punk rock came about because suddenly you could create a record for £100, and there was this explosive energy from people who could not play their instruments. With the arrival of digital technology and cheaper means of production I am surprised that there are not more "punk" film-makers. Writers should make scripts about edgier topics and try to understand themselves and their history and stop trying to suckle from the system. I include myself in that. For all I have said about structure, it is ultimately worthless without creativity. The three-act structure is the Big Mac of the movie world. The writer with a passion to tell a story is what I admire.

Writing is hard. You are abandoning your life, mentally and physically abstracting yourself outside of reality. At the same time, something on the lowest conscious level tells you, "Hey, you've only got 60 years to live, what are you doing stuck in a garret writing?" But when you really get into writing it becomes a meditation where you find a moment of stillness, or even change, within yourself.

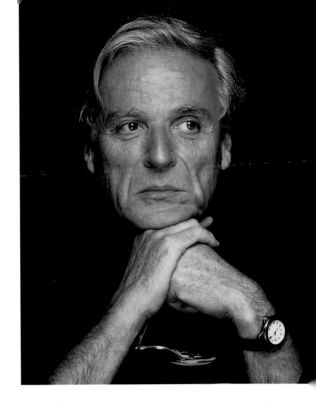

William Goldman was born in Highland Park, Illinois, in 1931. From the age of six he was hooked on the movies and was a regular visitor to his local cinema, the Alcyon Theater. He graduated from Oberin College, Ohio, in 1952 and after spending two years in the military he went on to receive a masters degree in English from Columbia University, New York, in 1956. That summer he wrote his first novel, 'Temple

william goldman

of Gold', in ten days. The book was published and Goldman's career as a novelist began. He did not start writing screenplays until 1965, with the script for **Masquerade** (Basil Dearden). He followed this with **Harper** (Jack Smight, 1966) which starred Paul Newman. Goldman had spent years researching the history of the Hole-in-the-Wall Gang before writing **Butch Cassidy and the Sundance Kid** (George Roy Hill, 1969). This script earned him an Academy Award. Goldman won a second for **All the President's Men** (Alan J. Pakula, 1976), adapted from the book by the two *Washington Post* journalists who exposed the Watergate scandal. From his own novels he adapted **Marathon Man** (John Schlesinger, 1976), **Magic** (Richard Attenborough, 1978) and **The Princess Bride** (Rob Reiner, 1987). He also adapted **A Bridge Too Far** (Richard Attenborough, 1977) and the Stephen King novel 'Misery' (Rob Reiner, 1991). He has a reputation for being one of Hollywood's most called-upon "script doctors", and of having helped rewrite countless screenplays uncredited. Goldman has authored 'Adventures in the Screen Trade', and 'Which Lie Did I Tell?'

interview

In my obituary you will read the line, "Nobody knows anything". Certainly I do not know what I am doing. If I did know, all the screenplays I wrote and all the movies I have been involved with would be wonderful, and that is clearly not the case.

When you are a screenwriter in Hollywood you write the selling version of a script. This is the version that will go to a studio head who will then decide if the script will be made into a film. He is the one who is going to say thumbs up or thumbs down. You have to remember the studio head is the enemy, and he is terrified of losing his job. What will make him lose his job is if he says yes to a lot of movies that lose a lot of money. All studio heads know they are going to be fired because they all are fired because they all make lots of movies that lose lots of money. The producer of a movie, who hires me, does not care so much if a movie is a flop, they care when they develop a movie and the movie does not happen. When you hire me now you are assuming that I am going to help you get the movie made. If I do not get the movie made, why pay me when you could get a young unknown writer who is much more malleable and much less expensive and much less wise-ass? The importance of the studio head is as true for me now as it was decades past when I started. From 1980 till 1985 the phone did not ring in my office – I wrote a lot of books in those five years, but I was a leper. This was not because I got stupid or got smart, the fact is I was the same person I had always been, except I wrote five screenplays that did not get made. Producers and studio executives therefore did not want to hire me.

Basically you write the selling version of the script to read as appealingly as you can make it. You want the studio head to read it and, hopefully, say, "Wait a minute, I can make money out of this". Most studio heads are very smart and very overworked and they tend to do their reading on weekends. They take home a shitload of scripts and all they want to do is finish reading them as quickly as they can so that they can get out and play golf or have drinks with friends. They are only going to read my script until they know they do not want to make it. That could be 10 pages or 50 pages. They are looking to say no because if they say no they have survived. If they say yes then the movie has to get made, all kinds of money has to be spent and the movie might be a flop.

To keep that studio head and ultimately the audience interested, I constantly throw in surprises and twists. I over-surprise; it is a huge flaw of mine, but I am trapped inside my own skin with my own inadequacies and I am terrified you're going to turn me off or stop reading me. I started as a novelist and I had a terror of you putting me down and saying, "I don't want to read this anymore". Therefore I want to have as many surprises as possible, as long as they are valid, so that the audience will say, "Oh my God I can't leave, I've got to finish this movie or book". I want them to say what a storyteller wants to hear most, which is, "What happens next?"

For example, in the middle of **Butch Cassidy and the Sundance Kid** I have a 29-minute chase where the two outlaws are followed by the superposse. Each time the outlaws tried to throw them off the trail the superposse would out-think them, out-fight them, out-something them, so that they would be in trouble again. That 29-minute chase is just this bunch of lawmen chasing Butch and Sundance, getting closer and closer, but they could never capture them because then I have got no story. So I had to keep it going, trying to write it as intriguingly as I could.

There is a chase in **Marathon Man** which illustrates one of the differences between movies and books. The hero, Dustin Hoffman, has just been terrorised by Laurence Olivier, and the bad guys are taking him out to kill him. In the novel from which I adapted the screenplay, there are three people who chase the hero – the first one has a limp and I figured even though the hero has been battered he can still outrun a guy who limps. When the limper can go no further, the second guy, who is a great big guy, goes after him. I figured logically the hero can outrun a great big guy if he has got enough of a lead. Then the third guy comes after him, and I gave the hero a huge lead so he could win that too. I did not want to have the audience say, "This guy has just been tortured, how can he beat anybody in a race?" However, in the movie none of that matters, Dustin Hoffman is running and men are chasing him. All the niceties that I stuck in to make it logical do not matter. You are seeing the city at night, you are seeing this kid in terrible pain, you are seeing the bad guys coming after

The TWO MEN are almost flying across the rocky terrain, never
losing balance, never coming close to stumbling; the battle
rages with incredible finesse, first one and then the other
gaining the advantage, and by now, it's clear that this isn't
just two athletes going at it, it's a lot more than that.
This is two legendary swashbucklers and they're in their
prime, it's Burt Lancaster in The Crimson Pirate battling
Errol Flynn in Robin Hood and then, incredibly, the action
begins going even faster than before as we

                                    CUT TO

INIGO, and behind him, drawing closer all the time, is the
deadly edge of the Cliffs of Insanity. INIGO fights and ducks
and feints and slashes and it all works, but not for long, as
gradually the MAN IN BLACK keeps the advantage, keeps forcing
INIGO back, closer and closer to death.

                    INIGO
              (happy as a clam)
          You are wonderful!

                    MAN IN BLACK
          Thank you - I've worked hard to
          become so.

The cliff edge is very close now. INIGO is continually being
forced toward it.

                    INIGO
          I admit it - you are better than I
          am

                    MAN IN BLACK
          Then why are you smiling?

Inches from defeat, INIGO is, in fact, all smiles.

                    INIGO
          Because I know something you don't
          know

                    MAN IN BLACK
          And what is that?

                    INIGO
          I am not left-handed

And he throws the six-fingered sword into his right hand and
immediately, the tide of the battle turns.

                                    CUT TO

The MAN IN BLACK, stunned, doing everything he can to keep
INIGO by the cliff edge. But no use.

Slowly at first, he begins to retreat. Now faster. INIGO is
in control and the MAN IN BLACK is desperate.

                                    CUT TO

INIGO, and the six-fingered sword is all but invisible now,
as he increases his attack, then suddenly switches style
again.

                                    CUT TO

A ROCKY STAIRCASE leading to a turret-shaped plateau, and the
MAN IN BLACK is retreating like mad up the steps and he can't
stop INIGO - and in a frenzy the MAN IN BLACK makes every
feint, every thrust, let's go with all he has left. But he
fails. Everything fails. He tries one or two final desperate
moves but they are nothing.

                    MAN IN BLACK
          You're amazing!

                    INIGO
          I ought to be after twenty years

And now the MAN IN BLACK is smashed into a stone pillar,
pinned there under the six-fingered sword.

                    MAN IN BLACK
              (hollering it out)
          There's something I ought to tell
          you

                    INIGO
          Tell me

                    MAN IN BLACK
          I am not left-handed either

And now he changes hands, and at last, the battle is fully
joined.

                                    CUT TO

Inigo. And to his amazement, he is being forced back down the
steps. He tries one style, and another, but it all comes down
to one thing - the MAN IN BLACK is in control. And before
INIGO knows it, the six-fingered sword is knocked clear out
of his hand.

                                    CUT TO

(1–6) "For **The Princess Bride** I had a
number of great sequences in my head but did
not know how I could join them together.
Then one day I was walking on the street
when I realised I could write the story as if my
father was reading it to me from an earlier
work. This meant I did not have to worry
about finding a reason to get from point A to
point B, because the narrator (my father)
simply said, there are 25 pages here that I am
not going to tell you about, and moved along
to the next part of the story." (1–2) An action
sequence from the script for the film.

A view of the SKY, AS PIECES OF PAPER MONEY flutter this way
and that in the breeze.

CUT TO:

BUTCH AND SUNDANCE, as Sundance starts to laugh.

                    SUNDANCE
          Think you used enough Dynamite
          there, Butch?

CUT TO:

The MONEY fluttering this way and that on the breeze. It
seems to fill the air. Then -

CUT TO:

The GANG starting off after the money, some of them crawling
across the ground, others are jumping into the air, trying to
catch the fluttering bills.

CUT TO:

BUTCH, starting to laugh at his own stupidity and

CUT TO:

The GANG, pursuing the money as it blows along. They might be
a convention of butterfly collectors, as they scramble
around, jumping and crawling and turning and -

CUT TO:

BUTCH, as slowly his laughter dies. He is looking off at
something.

CUT TO:

In the distance, a TRAIN ENGINE pulling one large, odd-
looking car.

CUT TO

BUTCH, still looking off at the engine and the single strange
car. SUNDANCE is beside him now, and they both watch. Around
them, members of the gang still scramble around, gathering up
bits and pieces of money.

CUT TO

THE ENGINE pulling the single car, drawing closer and closer
and

CUT TO

3

6

BUTCH and SUNDANCE watching it come.

                    BUTCH
          What the hell is that?

CUT TO

THE CAR, drawing closer, and now there is music under it all,
nervous and fast, but not loud, not yet, as the train and the
single car continue to come toward camera.

CUT TO

BUTCH and SUNDANCE looking at each other in absolute
bewilderment.

CUT TO

THE CAR. It is still some ways off, but the music is faster
now, as the camera picks up speed , moving toward the car,
which stands dead still on the tracks as the camera picks up
speed, moving toward the car and the car still waits and now
the music is starting to deafen, and CRAIG BREEDLOVE must be
driving the camera as it roars towards the car, close now,
really close, right up almost on top of the goddamn car and
just as it seems it's going to crash right into the side of
the car, the entire side of the car swings open and down, and
the camera recoils like a human face would recoil after
receiving a terrible blow, and out of the car right into the
eye of the camera comes riding - the SUPERPOSSE. The
superposse consists of perhaps half a dozen men. Taken as a
group, they look, act, and are, in any and all ways,
formidable.

CUT TO

BUTCH and SUNDANCE

                    BUTCH (CONT'D)
          Whatever they're selling. I don't
          want it (and he spins, shouting to
          the men gathering up the money) -
          leave it!

CUT TO

THE SUPERPOSSE riding like hell. They are still a good
distance away.

CUT TO

1

2

4

5

7

8

(1–8) "In this scene in **Butch Cassidy and the Sundance Kid** our heroes are chased by the 'superposse' for 29 minutes in the middle of the film. When the superposse first appears it is just a dumb railroad train. So I wrote a page of description building up that train (1–2). This dialogue is all me selling. I am trying to say to the studio head, who is my enemy as well as the man who can say thumbs up or thumbs down to me, that this is interesting, that it is going to work on movie screens all around the world and he can make money out of it."

4

(1–4) **Misery**: "When I adapt a novel I firstly read and re-read and re-read the source material. On each reading I mark what interests me with a different coloured pen (4). When I come to try and figure out what the story is I look at a page and if I see six different coloured marks on that page, I know that page is going to be in the movie. I turn to the next page and if there is no mark or one mark, I know that is not going to be in the movie. I am trying to locate the spine of the story. Once I have that spine I can write the movie, and until I have that I do not have any idea what I am going to do."

him and you want him to get away. I remember looking at that chase in the film, thinking all that work I did making it logical was ridiculous. In terms of the movie, it could have been any three guys chasing him. That is the difference between movies and books. The audience wants him to get away because he is Dustin Hoffman.

They like Dustin because he is a star and stars are very important in studio movies. Here is how that affects someone at my level (and by my level I don't mean high, because screenwriters are very low on the food chain in Hollywood – we have all been fired). Unless I write an original screenplay, which has not happened much lately, a producer sends me a book or an article. I will read it. If I think I can make it work and I really care for the material I will say yes. The producer will then make a deal with a studio. Producers never spend their own money, and so it is the studio which hires me. Then I will meet with the producer and he will say, "Kevin Spacey loves this book. Think of Kevin Spacey when you write the movie". Or, "Arnold Schwarzenegger loves this book, think of Arnold Schwarzenegger". I write what I can write, the producer will give it to the studio and then if they like it after rewriting and fiddling with it a little, they will then try and cast it. I am not very important. I may say, "Oh God don't go to that woman", or "please try him", but basically if they know that movie-star X is looking for a picture they will approach that star.

For example, years ago I wrote a comedy action film called **The Hot Rock** based on a wonderful novel by Donald Westlake. I wrote it for George C. Scott as an older crook and Robert Redford as his young cousin. The studio went to Redford first who liked it, but he did not want to play the young cousin. He felt the George C. Scott part was a better part, and so that was what he wanted to play. The older/younger aspect, which had been important in both the novel and the screenplay, was no longer valid because the movie was cast with Redford as the crook. It was not what I would have wanted in the first place, but that does not matter because the movie got made. And I cannot say for sure that if it had been George C. Scott and Redford the movie would have been any better.

If you look at the top ten movies of all time, only one had a movie star in it, and that was **Forrest Gump** and the star was Tom Hanks. There is no star in **Titanic**, there is no star in **Lord of the Rings**, there is no star in **E.T.**, and there is no star in **Star Wars**. They are group pieces. But for the studio that is hard to do, because they are taking a risk. The studios would much rather have the security of a major star. That means the writer had better write star parts. If you want to write for Hollywood you do not write Chekhov. You had better write parts where the studio can say, "Whoah, I can get Bruce Willis with this".

The studio also wants the security of having something optimistic at the end. All the time, you see movies that are going a certain way and then suddenly they get bullshitty in the last third. That is because the studios are saying, "We can't be negative, we can't be dark, we've got to give the audience something to hope for. Let's say the boy and the girl get together and the villain is destroyed".

In **American Beauty**, Kevin Spacey develops a fetish to sleep with this beautiful young girl. He loses weight, he changes his dress, God smiles on him, he is alone with her, they are on the couch and she will do what he wants. And guess what? He cannot sleep with her. That was not in the original script. That was the executives at Dreamworks saying, "Oh my God, it'll be a commercial flop if we have this". So they have Kevin Spacey say, "No, no, you're a virgin, I can't touch you". I absolutely hate that. But **American Beauty** was a gigantic worldwide success and is a critically honoured film. If I had done it, it would have been a disaster and no-one would have seen it. So the studio executives are the really smart ones and I am the asshole! They got it right for the mass audience, the mass audience did not want to see that little girl deflowered. That is an example of what you have to deal with when you are dealing with Hollywood films. It may drive us nuts, but the studios are very smart about a lot of what they do.

I was very wrong on a story called "Misery" based on a Stephen King novel of the same name. It is about a crazy woman who lives alone in Colorado with no-one else around. She rescues a man, who turns out to be her favourite writer in all the world, and keeps him prisoner. He has been crippled in an accident. He soon realises that this woman is violent. Gradually he gets out of the room in which she's holding him hostage, but she finds out about it. I remember when reading the novel I knew she was going to do something bad to him at this point, but I never dreamt she would do what she did. She cuts his feet off. This means he cannot move again. When I read that scene I thought, oh my God that is the most shocking, terrifying thing I have ever read. I essentially said yes to doing the movie so that I could write that scene and watch it with audiences right around the world. The producer/director, Rob Reiner, rewrote that scene so she did not cut his feet off. He had her break his ankles. I screamed

and said, no, you are destroying the movie. We did the movie his way, and at the first sneak preview when she breaks his ankles, the audience reaction was absolutely as horrific as you would want. They went with it and they hated her, but they loved the movie. If she had cut his feet off the audience would have hated her and hated the movie and we would have had a flop. I was wrong. A lot of the things that you think you are right about you are wrong about. Nobody really does know what will work. If we did, every book would be a bestseller and every movie would be a huge success, and they are not!

It is even more complicated to say what will work because you are trying to predict the future, and movies are very slow in the making. The fastest movie I was ever involved with was called **Maverick**. I delivered the script on 1 April 1993. Mel Gibson read it that week and liked it, which meant we were going to go ahead. And that same week Warner Brothers said we would come out the May holiday weekend, the following May. That is 13 months. We almost didn't make that, it was so hard to finish the film in just 13 months. Yet that is lightning for a movie. The point is a movie usually takes years between when you start and when it is released. One reason why nobody can tell what is going to work commercially is that you are trying to predict public taste, two, three, five years down the line and you cannot do that. It is basically impossible.

I am only talking about Hollywood films; I am not talking about what used to be called art films or independent films. That is a whole different world and I know nothing about that. I am only talking about studio films. If you want to make an inexpensive film you can tell different stories because the risks are not so terrible.

1

2

3

```
                WOODWARD (CONT'D)
        The whole U.S. Intelligence
        community is mixed in with the
        covert activities. The extent of it
        is incredible (little pause) And
        people's lives are in danger, maybe
        including ours.

                                CUT TO:

BRADLEE. He nods again, starts walking the two reporters back
to WOODWARD'S car.

                BRADLEE
        He's wrong on that last, we're not
        in the least danger, because nobody
        gives a shit - what was that Gallup
        Poll result? Half the country's
        never even heard the word
        Watergate.

                                CUT TO:

THE RED KARMANN GHIA as the three approach.

                BRADLEE (CONT'D)
        Look, you're both probably a little
        tired right?

They nod.

                BRADLEE (CONT'D)
        You should be, you've been under a
        lot of pressure. So go home, have a
        nice hot bath, rest up fifteen
        minutes if you want before you get
        your asses back in gear - (louder
        now) - because we're under a lot of
        pressure too, and you put us there
        - not that I want to worry you -
        nothing's riding on this except the
        First Amendment of the Constitution
        plus the freedom of the press plus
        the reputation of a hundred-year-
        old paper plus the jobs of the two
        hundred people who work here -
        (still building) - but none of that
        counts as much as this: you fuck up
        again, I'm gonna lose my temper.
        (pause, softer) I promise you, I
        don't want to lose my temper.
        (shoving them off) Move-move-move -
        what have you done for me tomorrow?
```

4

(1–4) **All the President's Men:** "It drives me nuts when people complain about films being inauthentic. **All the President's Men** was praised for being authentic in describing how the journalists Woodward and Bernstein uncovered President Nixon's involvement in the Watergate conspiracy. But I ended halfway through Woodward and Bernstein's own account of those events. I could not be authentic in the sense that a documentary could be, I could only be faithful in terms of tone – in other words, I did not put dancing girls in **All the President's Men** but I still altered the story a lot." (4) Excerpt from the film script of Bradlee, editor of the *Washington Post*, chastising the two journalists.

A WINDOWLESS ROOM

BABE is semi-conscious, wearing pajamas, damp. He sits in a
chair, the chair is in a windowless room. Babe blinks, tries
to get a better look at the place, but he's expertly bound to
the chair. The room seems unusually bright. There is a sink,
a table, it all seems clean.

There come SOUNDS from behind him and THE LIMPER and the
MOMMOTH walk around the chair. THE MAMMOTH carries an armload
of clean white towels, beautifully folded.

> LIMPER (ERHARD)
> Give me

He puts the towels on the table as we

> CUT TO

The BALD MAN moving toward the chair, carrying a rolled up
towel in one hand. He indicates that he wants a lamp brought
closer. THE LIMPER hurriedly obeys, the BALD MAN turns
quickly, washes his hands. As he does -

> BALD MAN
> (quietly)
> Is it safe?

> BABE
> (he wasn't ready for the
> question)
> Huh?

> BALD MAN
> Is it safe?

> BABE
> Is what safe?

> BALD MAN
> (his tone never changes;
> gently, patiently)
> Is it safe?

> BABE
> I don't know what you mean

> BALD MAN
> Is it safe?

> BABE
> I can't tell you if something's
> safe or not unless I know
> specifically what you're asking
> about

> BALD MAN
> (his hands are clean now;
> Erhard hands him a towel)
> Is it safe?

> BABE
> (rattled) Tell-me-what-the-"it"
> refers-to

> BALD MAN
> (softly as ever)
> Is it safe?

> BABE
> No, it isn't safe. Very dangerous,
> be careful.

For a moment the BALD MAN stares down at babe. There is a
terrible intelligence working inside. Now a nod. Just one,
that's all, and as he unwraps the towel he brought in we see
the contents: dental tools.

> CUT TO

ERHARD, bringing the lamp closer still and, as THE MAMMOTH
suddenly forces Babe's mouth open with his powerful hands -

> CUT TO

The BALD MAN. He selects an angled mirror and a spoon
excavator, not sharp, and leans forward toward Babe. He is
perspiring lightly and without a word THE LIMPER takes a
towel, dabs the BALD MAN's forehead dry. The BALD MAN is
concentrating totally on his work, and he is extraordinarily
skilled.

> CUT TO

Babe, helpless, while the BALD MAN gently taps and probes.
His hands move expertly here and there. Babe is perspiring
terribly. There is no sound in the room other than breathing.
The BALD MAN switches from the rounded spoon excavator to a
new tool, needle-pointed. Babe cannot stop sweating. The BALD
MAN shakes his head almost sadly.

> BALD MAN
> You should take better care of your
> teeth, there's a bad cavity here,
> is it safe?

> BABE
> Look, I told you before and I'm
> telling you now -

But that's all he has time for because the BALD MAN suddenly
shoves the needle pointed tool up the cavity and

> CUT TO

Babe, beginning to scream, but THE MOMMOTH cups his hands
over Babe's mouth, muffling the sound. When the scream is
done, he takes his hands away. Now the BALD MAN has picked a
small bottle, opened it, poured some liquid on his finger. He
brings the finger closer and closer to the cavity -

> BABE (CONT'D)
> - don't - please Jesus don't - I
> swear -

Now the finger is on the cavity and at first Babe starts to
wince but then after a moment he begins to almost lick the
finger; getting as much out of the liquid as he can, as if he
were a starving puppy and the BALD MAN was feeding him milk

The BALD MAN watches, not taking his finger away.

> BALD MAN
> Is it not remarkable? Simple oil of
> cloves and how amazing the results.

He pours some more on his finger; rubs it smoothly across
Babe's cavity.

> BALD MAN (CONT'D)
> Life can be, if only we allow it,
> so simple. (holding up the bottle)
> Relief. (holding up the explorer
> tool) Discomfort. (looking at Babe)
> Choose.

> BABE
> I can't satisfy ..what you
> want..because..because... (and now
> his tone changes)..aw no..no (and
> on those words-)

> CUT TO

The BALD MAN, his eyes expressionless, thrusting it home.
There is the start of a scream and the eyes look almost sad.
The scream continues, builds, abruptly stops and then -

> CUT TO

Babe in the chair, head slumped forward, semi-conscious, not
moving.

> CUT TO

3

(1–3) **Marathon Man**: "I have been to dentists in various countries, and
once they find out who I am they want to talk about that scene. Dentists'
offices are the only places where I am famous. As a kid I had a dentist who
did not believe in Novacaine and he really hurt me. It was very scary: you
are helpless and there is no pain like that of a tooth being removed. I can
still feel the pressure of his knee on my chest, as he was holding me in the
chair working on my teeth. Kids today, or in 20 years' time, may not be as
scared by this scene, because dentistry is so much better now and kids are
not as frightened of going to the dentist as they used to be." (4) "Once I
turned a corner at the Metropolitan Museum in New York and saw this
painting, and I was literally hit in the stomach by the power of it. It was El
Greco's 'View of Toledo', and it made me a better person, it made me a
more interesting person. Just as it makes me a better person to know what
Mozart could do. The wider the stuff that moves you, the more chance you
have of being able to move somebody else."

4

Storytelling is one of the basic parts of all of our lives. There is a line at the end of **Sunset Boulevard** where Gloria Swanson talks about all the little people out there in the dark, meaning all the people in movie theatres around the world. When we screenwrite we are trying to make memories for all of those people in the dark. I have written a couple of movies that people really responded to, and that thrills me. A friend told me that his little boy crawled on top of him and woke him up saying the line from **The Princess Bride** – "Hello, my name is Inigo Montoya, you killed my father, prepare to die". That made my month. It is just a fabulous thing that decades after I wrote a script I can affect a six-year-old kid so much that he would crawl up on top of his father and say that line.

biography

biography

Jean-Claude Carrière was born in 1931 in Languedoc. At the age of 24, having written one novel, he was approached by film-maker Jacques Tati to write book adaptations of Tati's films **Monsieur Hulot's Holiday (Les Vacances de M Hulot**, 1953) and **My Uncle (Mon Oncle**, 1958). Carrière was then conscripted to the Algerian War for two-and-a-half years. When he returned to France, Tati's assistant, Pierre

jean-claude carrière

Etaix, proposed that they make two short films together. One of them, **Happy Anniversary**, won an Academy Award. When the Spanish director Luis Buñuel was looking for a French collaborator for **The Diary of a Chambermaid (Le Journal d'une Femme de Chambre**, 1964), he chose Carrière. Buñuel was so pleased with his work that he then asked him to write **Belle de Jour** (1967). Carrrière's collaboration with Buñuel later included **The Discreet Charm of the Bourgeoisie (Le Charme Discret de la Bourgeoisie**, 1972) and **That Obscure Object of Desire (Cet Obscur Objet du Désir**, 1977). Carrière was also scriptwriter on **The Tin Drum (Die Blechtremmel**, Volker Schlöndorff, 1979), **Danton** (Andrzej Wajda, 1982), **The Unbearable Lightness of Being** (Philip Kaufman, 1987) , **Cyrano de Bergerac** (Jean-Paul Rappeneau, 1990) and on many other films. His theatre work includes French adaptations of the Indian epic 'The Mahabharata' and the Iranian epic 'The Conference of the Birds'.

interview

Every form of writing has attracted me. If I had lived in the 19th century the choice would have been between literature or the theatre. By the middle of the 20th century many new ways of writing had been invented. Firstly silent movies appeared, then recordings, then the talkies, followed by the radio, and then the TV. To have such an array of media to write for was unique in history, each one requiring a new and different way of writing. Cinema, which uses images, sounds and editing, was certainly a new technique and so it needed a new form of writing – screenwriting.

One distinctive feature of screenwriting is that a script is not a final piece of writing. It only really exists for the duration of the shoot. Then it disappears, its role complete. Scriptwriting is a kind of writing which has to vanish because a good script is one that gives birth to a good film. There is no such thing as a good script that gives birth to a bad film. If something is wrong in the film it was already wrong in the script. It is like the caterpillar and the butterfly; the caterpillar is a very clumsy animal but it contains all the elements, including the colours, of the butterfly. The moment the butterfly is born and flies away the dry skin of the caterpillar falls down to the ground, just as the script falls into the garbage can. The better the caterpillar, the better the butterfly and the longer the flight. As scriptwriter you must know as precisely as possible how what you write down on paper is going to become a film. What means will be used by the director, how much will it cost and how much time will it take? This knowledge is an intimate part of the screenwriter's job. The screenwriter who is unaware of these practicalities will face problems. When I started as a screenwriter I was lucky to be able to go through all the different technical crafts, working on the image, the sound and the editing.

Before I wrote any scripts I had already written two novels, one of which was published. I was 24. My publisher had a contract with Jacques Tati to publish books based on his films **Monsieur Hulot's Holiday** and **My Uncle**. Tati asked the publisher to get four or five young writers to each write a chapter and Tati would choose one to write the book. I was asked to write a chapter and it was picked. Going to visit Tati was my first contact with the movie world. When he answered the door I was very nervous and very impressed. He said, "I have read your chapter, I think it's fine, but what do you know about cinema?" I said, "Mr Tati, I go to the cinema two or three times a week and I have seen all your films four times. I love cinema", and he said, "No, no, that's not what I mean. What do you know about how to make a film?" I said "Well, I must confess I know nothing". So he called his editor and said, "Suzanne, take this young gentleman, and show him what cinema is". This lady took me to her small and dark editing room that was like a witch's cave. There she showed me this strange machine which allowed you to move the film

forwards and backwards and play with time. She put the first reel of the film onto the machine and the script beside her. She put her hand on the script and then showed me the film saying, "The whole problem is how to go from this (the script) to that (the film)". How to go from paper to the moving image. We worked for a week and that was my real initiation to the cinema. I asked, for example, why is it written in the script that the man enters the ocean, turns back and then looks right – and in the film he does not enter the ocean and looks left. Why is it different? The answer was usually practical – for instance the water was too cold or the actor was frightened. But the key reason for every change was that when Mr Tati was shooting he found out that it was a better way. He had the actors and he had the set, things that do not exist in the script. Every script is how the writer dreams a film. You can dream that you have every set you want and the best actors in the world including the dead ones, however when you shoot you have to make do with what you are given.

A script is already changing when you start finding the locations, designing the sets and casting the actors. Very often, once these visual elements are in place I would work on a script with the director just a few days before the shoot. The screenwriter must keep being flexible, always adapting to the story and to the way that the director works. In **Danton**, an important part of the script was that the two main characters, Danton and Robespierre, should meet only once. Before shooting we rehearsed this scene where they met, in [Andrzej] Wajda's apartment. The dialogue worked but there was some spark missing. I said to [Gérard] Depardieu (who played Danton), "I think there needs to be a physical contact between the two of you. Consider that it is easy for a judge to sentence someone to death but much more difficult to kill

I remember, I was eleven, I was
about to enter military school

(7–8) Stills of Luis Buñuel. "At the very beginning of his career when he wrote **Un Chien Andalou** with Salvador Dalí, Buñuel established a very interesting rule. If one writer proposes an image for a film, the other has no more than three seconds to either accept or reject that image. This prevents reason interfering. It either touches you inside or not. If you reject my idea I cannot defend it. We have to forget it forever and go to another idea. That is how we worked on **The Discreet Charm** for two years. When I first told Buñuel my idea for the surreal dinner scene in this film he rejected it and I could not defend it. Three months later I proposed it in a slightly different way and he still said no. Then when we introduced the dream to the film I suggested it again. This time he accepted. He said, 'When you offered it to me the first time it was too unreal, too impossible, but now with the dream in the film it works'." (1–6) One of several surrealist scenes from **The Discreet Charm**, where army officials smoke marijuana quite openly. (Following pages) Surrealistic images from Buñuel's **Un Chien Andalou**.

someone with his own hands. Now, what will you say to Robespierre?" Depardieu understood immediately. He took Robespierre's hand and put it round his neck saying, "You feel this flesh, this neck, if you keep going your way you will be obliged to cut it". This became one of the best moments in the film and it came from the collaboration with a great actor who gives more than he is asked for.

There are two types of writing. One is the literary way of writing a book. You can write a book alone, even publish it yourself. You put the words on paper and they do not change. No two readers will read the book in the same conditions, at the same speed, in the same place, stopping at the same pages etc. Each reader imagines the characters with different faces, sometimes identifying them with known actors. The second type of writing is for the performing arts. In that case, what you write is just the beginning of a technical process. Your words will be transformed and become something else at the end of that process. You will face not one reader but a group of people, an audience. They cannot stop or go back, they are obliged to go from the beginning to end at the pace you set. The process of writing is different, but so also is the process of receiving the result of your work.

If when writing, you think of how every word is going to be directed, it will paralyse you, restraining your inspiration and ideas. At some moment you must free yourself, and this ability to free yourself is a huge part of the craft of scriptwriting. I do it by writing in two separate "double movements" (as I call them). When I begin a story, I am at the crossroads of two, or ten, or even a thousand possibilities of actions. So I start the first part of my double movement by imagining myself as the first spectator of what I write. If I was

in a movie theatre and watching this film as a spectator, what would I love to see? What could happen? The second part of the first double movement is to forget about me being a spectator, and become one of the characters in the film. I enter the film and ask myself what would I do in this situation, how would I react? I am simultaneously spectator and character.

The second double movement involves proceeding in "waves". The first wave is the wave of exploration; I am at that famous crossroads and I have to explore all the different possibilities of action that exist without eliminating the improbable. Accepting everything takes a long, long time, because one crossroads leads to another crossroads, and once the characters do one thing that action leads to another range of choices. You have to explore and then go back and explore another possibility and the same again. It is very technical. The second wave is the wave of reflection, where I think over my choices. Maybe a certain idea was too much, perhaps it is interesting but maybe for another film in a few years from now. If you go only by waves of exploration you will end up with a story where anything is possible, without any logic. If you go only by waves of reflection, you will finish without anything surprising. It will all be prepared, logical and highly uninteresting.

The wave of reflection is necessary because the scriptwriter is never totally free in his choices. A film has to be carefully prepared and rehearsed. We know exactly what we are going to shoot, where and with which actor. So how do we make a "surrealistic" film which offers surprises, unexpected and unusual scenes or at least moments in a scene? Although film is a realistic medium made up of photographs, and a

(1–3) **Belle de Jour**: "I worked with Buñuel for 19 years, and each time we would go far from a city, in Mexico or in Spain, to a hotel somewhere, without our wives, without friends, just the two of us sharing the experience of being almost prisoners within the story. My best writing is done in partnership with the director. When you suggest something you can immediately see by the director's expression whether he feels deeply about it. You also overcome the loneliness of writing. Sometimes authors, including myself, are self-indulgent, and they are pleased by whatever they find, because it is their idea. Other writers behave the opposite way. They don't like anything they find and feel guilty."

We hear the sound of Charlotte beating him with the leather
scourge in the next room. The door opens off screen and Anais
comes in.

                    ANAIS
          Come on, there's someone waiting.

Severine leaves the spyhole with apparent regret and comes
towards the camera.

                    ANAIS (CONT'D)
          Well, did you see? What did you
          think of it?

                    SEVERINE
          How can anyone get so low…You must
          be used to it …But it disgusts me.

Anais looks at her enigmatically, thinking no doubt that
Severine does not see what sort of person she is herself.
Then she goes off and Severine follows her.

A bulky Asiatic has just arrived and is standing with
Mathilde in the entrance hall. The man opens a small Japanese
lacquered box which he is holding. (We do not see the
contents). He shows it to Mathilde. A curious humming noise
comes from inside the box. He looks at her interrogatively.
Repelled by it all, Mathilde replies in tones of considerable
disgust.

                    MATHILDE
          No thank you monsieur. Not for me.

Camera pans left as she goes off while the Asiatic closes the
box with a shrug. Anais and Severine come into view from the
left and camera pans back again as they go up to the Asiatic.
Anais introduces Severine, asking him -

                    ANAIS
          What about this one? Will she do?

Severine reaches up, puts an arm around his neck and kisses
him. The Asiatic looks at Severine, says something in an
Eastern language, then pulls a small white card of the
Diner's Club variety out of his pocket. He holds it out to
Anais.

                    ANAIS (CONT'D)
          What's this?

She takes out the card and examines it, then says in a
terrible English -

                    ANAIS (CONT'D)
          (reading) Credit card…Geisha's Club

She gives it back to the Asiatic and says loudly, trying to
make him understand with gestures -

                    ANAIS (CONT'D)
          No, no…it's no good here… (rubbing
          her thumb and forefinger together)
          Cash!

The man takes his card back. He nods, understanding, says
something and pulls out some banknotes. Anais takes two and
hands the rest back, saying to Severine -

                    ANAIS (CONT'D)
          All right, go ahead.

The Asiatic takes Severine, who kisses him. Holding her round
the waist, he comes with her towards us. We follow them as
they go off down the corridor to one of the bedrooms. He
pauses several times to kiss her on the neck. In contrast to
her previous manner, Severine seems to be looking forward
with enthusiasm to her work.

Medium shot inside the Blue Room. Severine enters, followed
by the Asiatic, who is still clutching his lacquered box. He
puts the box down on a chest of drawers, then takes off his
hat and coat and hangs them up. Then he advances towards
Severine. The same curious humming sound comes from it as
before. She looks down into the box and then looks up at the
Asiatic, rather alarmed. Smiling and firm, the Asiatic
gestures reassuringly and says in pidgin French-

                    ASIATIC
          Not to fear….Not to Fear

Then he continues to talk to her in his own language,
undressing as he does so. Severine puts down the box and
starts to take off her brassiere. The Asiatic objects volubly
and points to her briefs, indicating that she should remove
only them.

Medium close-up of the two of them from the waist up. The
Asiatic has now taken his shirt off, revealing an
impressively muscled body. Severine takes off her briefs and
hands them to the Asiatic, who has stretched out a hand. He
inspects the briefs, still chattering away, then raises his
arms. Severine strokes his shoulder appreciatively. In his
left hand he is holding a little bell, which he shakes.

Close-up of the Asiatic's face. Camera pans across to his
left hand as he shakes the bell, ringing it and talking at
the same time. Fascinated by this, Severine is watching him
intrigued. She breaks into a smile and suddenly draws the
Asiatic towards her, flinging her arms around his neck.

4

7

5

8

6

9

(3) 'The Robing of the Bride' by Max Ernst. "Mystery is the basis of surrealism. In any painting by Max Ernst or Yves Tanguey there is something which the viewer cannot understand. Similarly with the little box the Asiatic man shows the prostitutes in **Belle de Jour** (1–2, 4–9). We have absolutely no idea what is inside and we do not have to know. It is the reactions to it that are interesting – some people are attracted to it and others repelled. It is an irrational element in the storytelling, of which there are many in **Belle de Jour** since it is based on imagination and dreams as well as reality." (1–2) Extract from the screenplay of **Belle de Jour** published in English.

photograph is a moment of reality, the writer has to fight against that reality. It is much easier to be surreal on stage because the audience know that they are facing actors who do not really die when they fall down. However in the majority of films the more real the film looks the better it is regarded. Although difficult, the writer should try to introduce some elements of confusion into that reality and certainty.

When the American producer Saul Zaentz asked me to adapt Milan Kundera's book "The Unbearable Lightness of Being" many people told me it would be impossible to make a film from it. They said the book was a philosophical reflection that built up more like a piece of music than a standard plot. So I reread the book as a possible film, seeing if I could find the basis of a script hidden within. The story is about a couple, Tomas and Tereza, who leave Czechoslovakia after the Russian invasion and go to Switzerland. In Switzerland Tomas is unfaithful to Tereza, who has become totally bored. Tereza realises that she has lost the meaning of her life, which was to fight against the Russians, and so she returns to Czechoslovakia. The reader understands that she prefers to go back because the key elements influencing her decision are clear. Tomas is then left alone, but he is very happy. Although he loves Tereza, he does not love her all that much; he is successful in his work as a brain surgeon. One day he is alone in Geneva sitting at a café. It is a sunny day with beautiful light. Tomas cannot stand it for more than ten minutes and suddenly goes back himself to Czechoslovakia. This moment had all the qualities that we can ask from a story; it is unpredictable yet unavoidable at the same time. It says, simply by that one action, that Tomas loves Tereza more than he thought, that he loves Czechoslovakia more than he thought and that he loves darkness and maybe even death

more than he thought. When I read this I said to myself yes, there is a film there.

Each country should have its own cinema, just as it is vital that each country has its own painting and music. It would be terrible if there was only one type of music in the world. There is no one correct model of scriptwriting, but there is a dominant commercial model which comes from America. This American model produces a certain type of film. But it does not concern what we call cinema, because you can make films without making cinema, which is the case with the majority of the American film-makers. The pity would be that an African scriptwriter or an Iranian scriptwriter would try to write American films. That would be ridiculous. Cinema can be the expression of a people, of a nation, of a tradition. It is not a universal vehicle at all, nor should it be. How could an Iranian write an American film? Imagine a French publisher asking a Portuguese writer why they keep writing novels? "Buy French novelists, we have Balzac, Proust, Flaubert, and so on, and they are much better than yours. So read our books and stop writing your own novels". That is more or less what we hear from America regarding European films.

I say all the time to my friends in Africa to write films for an African audience, and to not pass over their brothers. A writer must speak his own language and start with his own market. Personally I have no interest in writing for an audience from the American Mid West. Why would I? From a commercial point of view it is absolutely logical to want your film to be seen by as many people as possible, but that is not the main purpose for someone who considers that cinema is an art form. The main purpose is to make good films. The milestones of cinema history are very rarely huge commercial hits.

jean-claude carrière

(1–13) "I worked on **The Tin Drum** not only because of the quality of the director and the original novel, but because it was my first film in Germany with a German director. This meant it opened doors for me to new people, new cities, new cultures and new ways of storytelling, because each country possesses its own culture of storytelling." Surreal imagination abounds in the film. The young Oskar Matzerath has not been able to grow since the age of three and can smash glass just by screaming (1–6).

2

3

4

Citizen Kane was not a success in America at all. An artist, wherever he is, starts by communicating with his own neighbours. They speak the same language, they face the same problems, they have the same history, they live in the same climate, they eat the same food and they love the same stories. If that artist subsequently goes all over the world, then so much the better.

Some of my friends, including American screenwriters, have their work schedule very well established for two or three years in advance. That to me is unthinkable. I do not know what I'm going to do in four months time. Of course I always have work for two or three months, you cannot survive otherwise, but being busy for one or two years would prevent me from accepting new and possibly fantastic adventures. As I always joked with my friends – I have to be ready in case Fellini calls! If you want fame you had better not only be a screenwriter, but if you want to have an interesting life going from one country to another country, from one time to another time, from one type of story to another type of story, then there is nothing like being a screenwriter. Much more than, say, a journalist for example, you can penetrate different cultures, countries, stories, times and places.

(1–4) "In **Danton** I had the opportunity to work with a Polish director, Andrzej Wajda, on the story of the French Revolution. I refused to do this with French directors because we would each be too involved, and come to it both having read the same books. In a similar way I explored the French bourgeoisie with the Spanish director Buñuel. It was challenging to have the ideas of a foreigner on my own tradition and culture."

biography

Born in 1912 to a farming family in Hiroshima, Kaneto Shindo is one of cinema's most prolific screenwriters, with over 200 scripts to his credit. Shindo started in the film industry in 1933 as an assistant art director working with Akira Kurosawa among others. In 1937 he won a film magazine competition with his first script. Shindo then refined his craft by working as an apprentice writer to

kaneto shindo

celebrated Japanese director Kenji Mizoguchi until 1943 when he was drafted into the Japanese navy to fight in the Second World War. Once the war finished Shindo returned home to work as a scenarist with the major Japanese studio Shochiko. He left it in 1950 to form his own company Kindai Eiga Kyokai along with director Kimibasuro Yoshimura. The company has since become one of the most respected independent production companies in Japan, its work often distinguished by political concern and social awareness. Shindo made his directing debut in 1951 with **My Beloved Wife (Aisai mono Gatari)** and has since directed over 30 of his own screenplays while continuing to write numerous scripts for many other directors. His 1960 film **The Island (Hadaka no Shima)** was scripted without any dialogue and went on to win the Moscow International Film Festival Grand Prix. Other films he has scripted and directed include **Children of Hiroshima (Gembaku no Ko**, 1953), **Onibaba** (1964), **Kuroneko** (1968), **A Last Note (Goyo no Yuigon-jo**, 1995) and **Will to Live (Ikitai**, 1998). He is the honorary chairman of the Japanese Screenwriters Association.

interview

Nothing interests me apart from people and the way in which people live. A long time ago, Japan went to the continent of China and started a vicious war. The Japan that went to China and started a war was the same Japan that suffered an atomic bombing from the US. The US pilot who pushed the button that opened the bomb bays, and those Japanese who had the radiation thrown on them were all equally human. People are both the devil and God and are truly mysterious. A surgeon can cut people open and take them apart but a surgeon cannot disassemble their real heart. When I say "heart" I am not talking about the physical organ but rather something intangible that resides within us – something which doctors cannot see or analyse. I want to do what doctors cannot do.

Who does a writer write about? He writes about himself. When I began writing at 25 years of age I did not realise this. I wanted to write about subjects that excited my own curiosity. But the more I wrote the more I came to realise that I was writing about myself. I do not know what my closest friend is thinking. I do not know anyone else's mind, but I do know

原爆の子

近代映画協会 共同製作
劇団 民芸

北星映画株式会社・配給

London Times'—
"This film deserves
the widest possible
publicity."

CHILDREN OF HIROSHIMA
("ATOM BOMB CHILDREN")
Internationally Acclaimed Film from Japan

1

2

3

4

5

6

"Throughout history terrible things have happened; yet people manage to pass around these difficulties and move forward, displaying an inherent ability to survive. That is my overriding theme. In that context one of my preoccupations is the atomic bombing. I am from Hiroshima and members of my family were exposed to the bomb and had radiation sickness. I believe that in the 21st century nuclear power is the most important issue facing humanity. As the very first city to suffer the devastation of atomic power, I think Hiroshima has a right to address the world." Shindo wrote five films about the bombing including **Children of Hiroshima** (1–4, 6), which tells the story of a kindergarten teacher who returns to the city and meets some of the young survivors. The film stresses the contemporary life of the survivors rather than the destruction of the city. (5) Still of the devastation in Hiroshima following the atomic bombing.

who I am. I know what kind of evil thoughts I have. I know what kind of good thoughts I have. Furthermore, I know that within my own heart those thoughts are constantly at battle. So when I write I seek themes that represent myself, and the process of writing becomes an internal battle with myself.

Stories evolve from problematic situations. Once a problem arises, the story begins. Something must happen to make it a story, but nothing should happen simply for the sake of the story. The characters create the story. For some writers it is like the case of the chicken and the egg – they ask themselves which comes first, the protagonists or the story? I feel that characters come first and the story is subordinate. If you begin with a story then the roles of the characters will be fixed, which is not true to life. We have moved on from the time when people exist for the sake of stories. We have gone beyond that. We have now entered a period when stories flow forth from people.

There was a time in America when it was thought that you could create a production line to manufacture scripts. There were different people in charge of different aspects of a script. The idea was that their various talents would come together and that the sum of the parts would be greater than any one individual's contribution. However, it was discovered that such a system does not work. A group of writers creates friction and the sum becomes smaller than the parts. We are each unique, we all have our own individuality and every one of us is blessed with great talent. Unless we build upon these distinctive characteristics, there can be nothing original. It is the author's mind, individuality and personality that creates the script.

My own background is that I was born as a farmer into a big family on the coast of the inland Sea of Seto (west Japan). I grew up watching my parents' hard labour in the fields, particularly the figure of my mother carrying a heavy burden on her bent back. I remember the rice planting at the beginning of summer, followed by mowing under the burning sun and then the busiest harvest season in autumn. When I thought of all this later it seemed very symbolic to me. So in 1960 I wrote and directed a film called **The Island**. In the film, there is a couple with two children who live on an island, who have to bring water from another island nearby. They need water for consumption, cooking and for agricultural purposes. The story describes the process of fetching that water every day. The land is quite coarse. They throw water on the dry land, and the water seeps into the landscape. Again they put water on the land, it seeps in again, and they put it on again. For me, the dried land is the human heart. The story came from my own individual experience.

The Island is a talkie movie, but there is no dialogue and the drama develops through images. You can only hear the wind, the sea and the indistinct sound of voices. When I was a child, it was difficult for the farmers to express their fight with the earth. I wanted to express the farmers' feeling of silence. So in **The Island** I decided to show the reality of farming life in a kind of visual poem. As I wrote the script it then became an experiment in how to create drama and conflict without dialogue. The image became the narrator. The images of every shot and scene conflict with each other and through this conflict the image creates drama. I believe that screenwriters write to create images. Film is all about images. Dialogue is not the primary driving force in cinema. Scenarists are not novelists because although they do write text, the ultimate

A young woman is beating clothes on a stone with a stick.
This rhythmic beating continues throughout the scene. A man
approaches.

                MAN
          A fine day.

                YOUNG WOMAN
          You've caught a big fish.

                MAN
          I had nothing to eat - how do you
          manage? You don't seem to grow
          anything.

The woman doesn't reply. He approaches her.

                MAN (CONT'D)
          Do you steal? That's it. Everyone
          steals in Kyoto and anywhere there
          is fighting. So you steal too?

She turns to the man, angry from his insinuations.

                YOUNG WOMAN
          Why didn't you save my husband?

He answers her question directly.

                MAN
          There wasn't time. Twenty farmers
          attacked the two of us. All I could
          do was get away.
              (beat) You must have been waiting
          for him. What will you do now? He's
          dead. No use staying with the old
          woman.

                YOUNG WOMAN
          It's none of your business.

                MAN
          You're still young. How about
          coming to me.

He looks at her lustfully. Through the reeds, her mother-in-
law approaches. She stops and looks at both her daughter-in-
law and the young man. Both look at her.

                MAN (CONT'D)
          A fine day.

The Mother-in-law first looks at her daughter-in-law, and
then asks the young man -

9

                MOTHER-IN-LAW
          What are you doing here?

                MAN
          I've been fishing. I've got food
          to eat. You have it.

He throws his fish to the young woman. She looks at her
mother-in-law, undecided whether or not to accept the fish.

                MOTHER-IN-LAW
          Take what's offered.

She takes the fish. The man leaves.

                MOTHER-IN-LAW (CONT'D)
          What did he say?

                YOUNG WOMAN
          Nothing.

                MOTHER-IN-LAW
          He's no good. He's not even sorry
          he came back alone. He may have
          killed my son. Don't be too
          friendly with him.

(1–12) **Onibaba**: Transcript and frames from a
scene in **Onibaba** exploring the relationship
between the mother-in-law and her son's wife
(1–8), who kill Samurai to survive. In this
scene, the women meet a man who later
claims to be a 'friend' of the mother's son. In
Onibaba, the mother-in-law wears a mask to
frighten her daughter-in-law (12) just as in the
Japanese legend that inspired Shindo when
writing the script for the film.

3

4

5

6

7

8

10

11

12

screenwriting

product is not text. I may use characters in my writing, but what I am ultimately seeking to create is image. If you are unable to imagine those final images in your mind you should not be a screenwriter.

Film does have a mission to be entertaining, but it is not simply a matter of making movies that are purely entertaining. It is important to write scripts which give us an inspiration to live. Sometimes my own films are misunderstood because they are interpreted as expressions of sex or expressions of violence. This happens when the audience fails to dig deeper. The story is not about the sex or the violence but the investigative act of considering what sex is or what violence is. That is why you make the movie. I used sex as my theme in a movie I wrote and directed called **Onibaba**. I also borrowed a small element from an old Japanese story for this film.

In that Japanese story, there is a young woman and her mother-in-law, and the young woman wants to go to a Buddhist temple. In order to prevent her from going the mother-in-law puts on a devil's mask and ambushes her on her way. On seeing this devil's mask the young woman is frightened and runs home. The mother-in-law is then punished by God and becomes unable to remove the mask. That legend is drawn from the Japanese Buddhist law that states: "Thou shalt not stand in the way of someone who is going to pray at a temple". The script for **Onibaba** is similar in that there is also a young woman who lives with her mother-in-law. The young woman's husband (the mother-in-law's son) was a Samurai who has been killed in battle. However, instead of the woman's destination being a Buddhist temple,

in **Onibaba** I made the destination a man. The woman is going to this man in order to sleep with him. To prevent her from going the mother-in-law puts on a horrific mask and frightens the woman on her way to meet him. This continues until the mask becomes stuck to the mother-in-law. This part I borrowed from the Japanese legend.

In Japan there is a tradition of storytelling. In the past storytellers would stand on a street corner and just talk. This developed into modern theatre and then into movies and now TV. It is all an extension of storytelling, of speaking to people. **Onibaba** is set in the 16th century during the warring states period in Japan when the Samurai were fighting. In our world there are often wars and as a result people suffer, but they manage to persevere, have sex, procreate and carry on. That is the history of humanity: the story of procreation, sex and carrying on.

I had the chance to study scriptwriting before the war by serving as an apprentice to the director Kenji Mizoguchi, just when Japanese movies became talkies. At that time the company had a separate division responsible for writing so there were several veterans, and underneath these veterans there were apprentices like me. After the war the scenario division inside the company was abolished and the company made freelance contracts with the scenarists on a casual basis. It was a great way to learn. It's quite, quite simple (and you don't get paid)! You go and you write a script, the veterans look at it and evaluate it and criticise it for you, and that is a process that is repeated again and again. If the veterans who are reviewing your work are not brilliant it does not go well. Fortunately Mizoguchi was brilliant, both as a critic and as a director, and therefore I benefited greatly from that

2

3

4

5

6

(1) Shindo directing. "My work is moulded by the legacy of the great writers, and that transcends national, linguistic and cultural barriers. Although these masters have great dialogue and great situations, you are never allowed to steal from them, rather their inspiration flows through my blood without me really understanding how it is expressed. Shakespeare, Molière (5), Chekhov (6), Eugene O'Neill, Tennessee Williams are all in my blood, as are the ancient Japanese traditions and legends. The world is also full of great movies. Those film-makers who passed before me, and who were much more talented than I, also created a great legacy for me to learn from. Japanese movies grew through the benefit of American, French and Italian movies. Directors like John Ford and Billy Wilder had a great influence on Japanese film-makers. But in Japan we have our own traditions and our own traditional arts, and that is why we do not try and imitate European or American films. We try and learn from their techniques and use those techniques to develop our own cinema." (2) Still from Ford's **Stagecoach** and (3) Wilder's **Some Like it Hot**. (4) 'Kamezo as the Warrior Monk', a painted pen and ink drawing from 1856 by the Japanese artist Utagawa Kunisada.

During his eighties, Shindo's films have explored the theme of old age. **A Last Note** (1, 4) is the story of an ageing actress who visits her villa in the country for the summer and ends up returning to Tokyo to work on the stage. "The lead actress Haruko Sugimura is over 80 but spry and fit and spends most of her time acting. To her, life is working. People who have lost their thinking capacity owing to senility must be cared for by the government. Healthy normal people want to think and behave actively because that is the purpose of human beings. On this earth, only man is creative. The inhabitants of this world must not end their years merely in a daze." (2–3) "When I came to write **The Island** I took all of the characteristics that one finds in humanity and I used those characteristics in the four characters of one wife, one husband and two children. Through them I expressed the great problems that we all deal with." (5) One of the many books Shindo has authored, featuring his scripts and thoughts on the craft of scriptwriting.

experience. Although now the contractual relations are a freelance system, it is still generally the case that young aspiring scenarists work closely with an established veteran.

When writing a script there are ways to write dialogue, to construct the story, to express movement, and many other specific details which I had to learn, but fundamentally it is the complete film which is my master. Many of the films made by Hollywood and in Britain, France and Russia, are like masters that teach me. What is important is to incorporate the essence of those great masters into my own work without merely imitating them. Nobody comes out of the womb as a screenwriter. It takes great effort to develop such talent. There are skills to learn, but it is not something you go to school and learn. You have to be a talented artist, you have to learn about people, about cinematic technique and about writing, and unless your ability to understand cinematic technique matches your ability to write, it will not work out.

Every aspiring writer needs to gain experience, and experience comes from effort. Through effort you also improve ability. The thoughts and ideas in our minds are without structure, and in order to give them structure we need skill. To get skill you have to study. Study, study and study. Aspiring writers must know that. The writer should always be satisfying his curiosity. Curiosity should be boundless. What you do not know, treat as a challenge. Remember that all our lives do not go along smoothly without incident. As you live through life you come up against barriers and obstacles. What is important is that you get over these problems. You fall down but then you get back up, and you try different ways and experiment. Soon you are going to fail once again, and then you are going to have to get up again. Your talent will not

blossom unless you learn how to recover from your downfalls. What is very important in becoming a screenwriter is to understand when you have fallen down. Many people do not.

I have enjoyed my work as a writer and my life has been enriched by it. People do all kinds of work. Some people make movies, other people make chairs. Everybody works, but unless you enjoy your work it does not go well. If you are not interested it will not be good. But if you are interested in your work you dig deeper; you really dig and dig and dig and you get better at it. Unless you do this you will not be able to move anybody else by it. As you continue to explore your work and your life the more you will realise that you do not know everything. The only thing worth living for is that there is always something new to learn. Do not despair – the only reason I carry on after 89 years of life is because there is still more to know. And if you ever feel like you know it all, then you will just simply die. So, keep digging!

Ruth Prawer Jhabvala was born in Cologne in 1927 and has been writing since the day she learnt the alphabet. Her parents were Jewish and as a result she was forced by Nazi regulations to attend segregated schools. In 1939 Jhabvala and her family fled Germany and the Holocaust, finding refuge in England. At 24, after receiving her masters degree from London University, Jhabvala moved to Delhi where she

ruth prawer jhabvala

began her prolific career as a novelist. Jhabvala had no interest in cinema until director James Ivory and producer Ismail Merchant bought the rights to her novel 'The Householder' in 1960, and asked her to write the film script adaptation. That was the beginning of her collaboration with Merchant Ivory which has lasted over 40 years. Early films include **Shakespeare Wallah** (1965) and **Autobiography of a Princess** (1975). Working closely with James Ivory, Jhabvala identified an affinity between his sensibility and that of novelists E. M. Forster and Henry James; from James she adapted **The Europeans** (1979), **The Bostonians** (1984) and **The Golden Bowl** (2000); and from Forster **A Room with a View** (1985) and **Howards End** (1992), both of which gained her an Academy Award. Jhabvala received an Oscar nomination for her adaptation of Kazuo Ishiguro's novel 'The Remains of the Day' (1993). She has continued to write novels, and adapted her own work, 'Heat and Dust', in 1982.

This is the way I set about adapting a book: I read it once, twice, three times and then I put it away. After that I work without the book for a bit. I have to find a form that is **not** that of the novel, the form of the film is **never** that of the novel. This form is a sort of construct in my mind. It is very difficult to describe. It is easier to describe the difference between writing a novel and writing a screenplay. When I write a novel, I don't really have an idea in which direction or in what manner it is progressing. It has to be allowed to grow. But with a screenplay (an original as well as an adaptation) I must know from the start in which direction it has to go. By that I don't mean the progress of a story from beginning through middle to end. It is more a concept of what would best express the essence of the film. For instance, the film **Mr. & Mrs. Bridge** was based on two novels by Evan Connell that are written as a series of short sketches. I used these sketches but in a different form. This form was the progress of the seasons: the film starts off in spring and ends in deepest winter, not of one year but of a succession of years during which the parents grow old and the children grow up. So the form of the film has

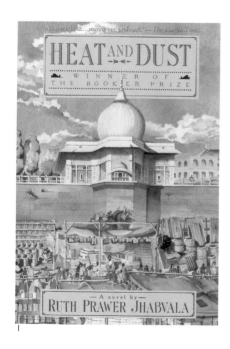

"I have written about 20 films but I am still primarily a fiction writer. It is writing fiction which has made me at home in an editing room, because for years and years I have done in my novels what an editor does to a film – cutting, compressing, shifting scenes around for more effective contrast or counterpoint. It works the other way around too. I wrote 'Heat and Dust' (1) in a linear way, with the contemporary (3) and the 1923 story (2) as separate entities: then I cut the whole thing up so that the two different time periods correlated with one another, the way we would have done in a film. My subsequent novels are written in a way that would have made them easy to cut and recut in an editing room. Two of my novels, 'In Search of Love and Beauty' and 'Shards of Memory', are composed of a series of juxtaposed scenes, which move around freely in time and space like a series of flashbacks joined together."

become the course of human life, which is reflected in the course of the seasons.

It is only when I have some conception, however vague, of the form (which is not the structure) that I can begin to focus on the content. At this point my method of working can vary. Much of it depends on how much time there is before I turn the screenplay in (or surrender it, as I tend to think). Sometimes I have to do what is really a rush job. For example on **Hullabaloo**, Merchant Ivory had to have a script in a matter of weeks, in fact they were already on location before I had finished writing it. But if I have a lot of time then I do like to prepare more elaborately and go through many different versions. If I love a project that will make a difference. I must confess that this has not always been the case. There have been instances when I have not been very keen on the project in hand, yet knowing that we had to have a script I wrote it cold, almost like an exercise, like one might solve a problem in chess or maths. That is a different kind of enjoyment, the pleasure of using one's technical skill.

But when I love a project I do spend as much time on it as I can. My two favourite adaptations have been **Mr. & Mrs. Bridge** and **The Golden Bowl**. I set about doing both of them the same way: through analysis. Going through the books, I made a separate analysis of each character, marking their individual characteristics. So I might have a heading for appearance; for turn of speech; for simplicity; for complexity; for integrity; for deviousness; for selfishness; for altruism and so on, running the whole gamut of human personality and passions. Of course this can only be done with the greatest books where the characters are real, complex and leap at you off the page. I also had headings for the relationships of the characters with one another, marking passages where they seem to love one another, where they can't stand one another, where they put up with one another. This can go on indefinitely, since it applies not only to each character with one other but each character with everyone. There are endless cross-references and entanglements. That is really fun.

If there is time I read a lot around the project, although the moment the project is finished I completely forget everything I learned. For a while (while reading about **Jefferson in Paris**) I became a little expert on Jefferson and American slavery and the French revolution. I can't dignify this reading as research, it is just reading around a subject and as much as possible of what has been written or recorded about it. For something set in the past I like to read books contemporary with the project, in order to feel my way into it. With authors I admire, like [Henry] James and [E. M.] Forster, I would want to read not only all their own novels but also those of their contemporaries, and their biographies in great detail. One thing I don't read is literary criticism – that is, other people's interpretations of their work, which I feel is none of my business while I am struggling with my own.

While I have the greatest reverence for some books, I feel that in turning them into a film it is necessary to be absolutely irreverent. At that stage, it is only the screenplay that matters, and getting that screenplay to work is my sole concern. I have no compunction about radically changing scenes or inventing new ones. Sometimes what works triumphantly in a book does not work at all in a film. **The Golden Bowl** is a prime example. The novel is told entirely obliquely, with nothing stated directly but only by hints, guesses, flashes. Nothing is explicit, but my goodness what a lot is implied. The film had

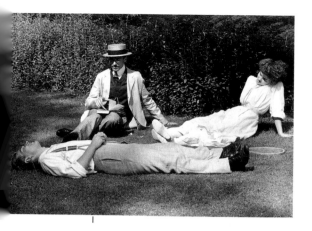

(1) Still from **A Room with a View** of the scene in which Cecil (Daniel Day-Lewis) reads to Lucy Honeychurch (Helena Bonham-Carter). (2–4) The same scene in the screenplay and in the novel (5–7).

CECIL
(reading louder, not liking any
interruption) "Under Orcagna's
Loggia - the Loggia de'Lanzi, as
we sometimes call it now - "

LUCY
What's the title?

CECIL
(reading from spine) Under the
Loggia by Eleanor Lavish.

LUCY
(bursting into laughter) Eleanor
Lavish! Oh my goodness! Mr.
Emerson, you remember Miss Lavish?

GEORGE
Of course I do.

LUCY
No wonder the novel's bad. But
I suppose one ought to read it as
one's met her.

His dark head is very near her lap. She stares down at
it. We feel her impulse could be to suddenly stroke it.

CECIL
There's an absurd account of a
view which I will spare you -

LUCY
No, do read it...How do you like
our view, Mr. Emerson?

GEORGE
My father says there's only one
perfect view -

He looks up into her face - She waits, interested.

GEORGE
- the view of the sky straight
over our heads, and that all
these views on earth are bungled
copies of it.

CECIL
(shutting the book with a snap)
I expect your father has been
reading Dante.

He gets up, ready to stalk off.

2

struck her that she could mean something else. She watched his head, which was almost resting against her knee, and she thought that the ears were reddening. 'No wonder the novel's bad,' she added. 'I never liked Miss Lavish. But I suppose one ought to read it as one's met her.'

'All modern books are bad,' said Cecil, who was annoyed at her inattention, and vented his annoyance on literature. 'Everyone writes for money in these days.'

'Oh, Cecil – !'

'It is so. I will inflict Joseph Emery Prank on you no longer.'

Cecil, this afternoon, seemed such a twittering sparrow. The ups and downs in his voice were noticeable, but they did not affect her. She had dwelt amongst melody and movement, and her nerves refused to answer to the clang of his. Leaving him to be annoyed, she gazed at the black head again. She did not want to stroke it, but she saw herself wanting to stroke it; the sensation was curious.

'How do you like this view of ours, Mr Emerson?'

'I never notice much difference in views.'

'What do you mean?'

'Because they are all alike. Because all that matters in them is distance and air.'

'H'm!' said Cecil, uncertain whether the remark was striking or not.

'My father' – he looked up at her (and he was a little flushed) – 'says that there is only one perfect view – the view of the sky straight over our heads, and that all these views on earth are but bungled copies of it.'

'I expect your father has been reading Dante,' said Cecil, fingering the novel, which alone permitted him to lead the conversation.

'He told us another day that views are really crowds – crowds of trees and houses and hills – and are bound to resemble each other, like human crowds – and that the power they have over us is something supernatural, for the same reason.'

Lucy's lips parted.

177

LUCY
...Cecil, do read the description
of the view.

CECIL
Not while Mr. Emerson is here
to entertain us.

LUCY
No - read away. Nothing's funnier
than to hear silly things read out
loud. If Mr. Emerson thinks we're
frivolous, he can go help look for
tennis balls.

CECIL is pleased with this reply and sits down again,
mollified.

LUCY
Mr. Emerson, go and find tennis
balls.

GEORGE
Must I?

LUCY
No, of course not.

CECIL
(yawning, handing the book to
LUCY) It's in Chapter 2 - just
find me Chapter 2.

LUCY leafs through the book to find the chapter. She
reads something which freezes her. Her eyes are
stretched wide.

CECIL
Here - give it to me.

LUCY
(holding the book away from him)
Oh it's too silly - who would
want to read such rubbish -

CECIL reaches over and takes the book from her and reads:

CECIL
"Afar off the towers of Florence,
while the bank on which she sat
was carpeted with violets. All
unobserved, he stole up behind
her" - isn't it immortal? - "there
came from his lips no wordy
protestations such as formal
lovers use..."

3

He looks up from the book to have her share his smile -
Afraid of what he might see in her eyes, she turns them
from him -

And looks straight into GEORGE's, unblinkingly raised
to hers -

CECIL
"No eloquence was his, nor did
he suffer from the lack of it.
He simply enfolded her in his
manly arms - " This isn't the
passage - there's another much
funnier further on - (searching
for it)

LUCY
(in a steady voice) Should we
go in to tea?

She rises and leads the way.

CECIL
By all means, tea rather than
Eleanor Lavish.

He follows her.

GEORGE follows them both. They enter the shrubbery.

CECIL
Oh, I forgot the book -

LUCY
Never mind -

CECIL
It's your mother's library book
and she will fuss.

He goes back to get it.

GEORGE blunders against her in the narrow path.

LUCY
No -

But he kisses her (on the lips).

And she stands still for him.

CECIL'S VOICE can be heard approaching - "I must read
you the bit about the murder - a crime passionel - "

LUCY walks on.

4

'For a crowd is more than the people who make it up.
Something gets added to it — no one knows how — just as
something has got added to those hills.'

He pointed with his racquet to the South Downs.

'What a splendid idea!' she murmured. 'I shall enjoy
hearing your father talk again. I'm so sorry he's not so well.'

'No, he isn't well.'

'There's an absurd account of a view in this book,' said
Cecil.

'Also that men fall into two classes — those who forget
views and those who remember them, even in small rooms.'

'Mr Emerson, have you any brothers or sisters?'

'None. Why?'

'You spoke of "us".'

'My mother, I was meaning.'

Cecil closed the novel with a bang.

'Oh, Cecil — how you make me jump!'

'I will inflict Joseph Emery Prank on you no longer.'

'I can just remember us all three going into the country
for the day and seeing as far as Hindhead. It is the first thing
that I remember.'

Cecil got up: the man was ill-bred — he hadn't put on his
coat after tennis — he didn't do. He would have strolled
away if Lucy had not stopped him.

'Cecil, do read the thing about the view.'

'Not while Mr Emerson is here to entertain us.'

'No — read away. I think nothing's funnier than to hear
silly things read out loud. If Mr Emerson thinks us frivolous,
he can go.'

This struck Cecil as subtle, and pleased him. It put their
visitor in the position of a prig. Somewhat mollified, he sat
down again.

'Mr Emerson, go and find tennis balls.' She opened the
book. Cecil must have his reading and anything else that he
liked. But her attention wandered to George's mother, who
— according to Mr Eager — had been murdered in the sight
of God and — according to her son — had seen as far as Hindhead.

6

'Am I really to go?' asked George.

'No, of course not really,' she answered.

'Chapter two,' said Cecil, yawning. 'Find me chapter
two, if it isn't bothering you.'

Chapter two was found, and she glanced at its opening
sentences.

She thought she had gone mad.

'Here — hand me the book.'

She heard her voice saying: 'It isn't worth reading — it's
too silly to read — I never saw such rubbish — it oughtn't to
be allowed to be printed.'

He took the book from her.

' "Leonora," ' he read, ' "sat pensive and alone. Before
her lay the rich champaign of Tuscany, dotted over with
many a smiling village. The season was spring." '

Miss Lavish knew, somehow, and had printed the past
in draggled prose, for Cecil to read and for George to
hear.

' "A golden haze," ' he read. He read: ' "Afar off the
towers of Florence, while the bank on which she sat was
carpeted with violets. All unobserved, Antonio stole up
behind her — " '

Lest Cecil should see her face she turned to George, and
she saw his face.

He read: ' "There came from his lips no wordy pro-
testation such as formal lovers use. No eloquence was his,
nor did he suffer from the lack of it. He simply enfolded her
in his manly arms." '

There was a silence.

'This isn't the passage I wanted,' he informed them.
'There is another much funnier, further on.' He turned
over the leaves.

'Should we go in to tea?' said Lucy, whose voice remained steady.

She led the way up the garden, Cecil following her,
George last. She thought a disaster was averted. But when
they entered the shrubbery it came. The book, as if it had
not worked mischief enough, had been forgotten, and Cecil

179

7

to work the other way around and turn what was so deeply implicit in the novel into scenes where people attempt to explain their extremely complicated feelings.

As for dialogue, it is a tricky business to turn literary dialogue into its cinematic equivalent. When the former appears to be at its most colloquial, it is often at its most literary – in fact the most expressive dialogue in a book *is* literary, reflecting the art of the novelist. But try and put this dialogue directly into the mouth of an actor and it will sound stilted – not art, but artifice. To sound colloquial film dialogue has to be a lot more stark than it is in a novel. And one must never forget that added to the words on the page of a script is the entire range of expression brought to the screen by the appearance, manner and personality of the actor speaking those words.

Calculating the amount of dialogue necessary to write has given me a lot of headache. In my first screenplay, "The Householder" I had no idea that far fewer words were needed than in the novel, and I wrote reams of dialogue in the same way as I would for a novel. I quickly found that most of it had to be thrown out. Later on, trying to learn, I went in the opposite direction and wrote far too few words. Two of our earlier films, **The Guru** and **Bombay Talkie**, just don't have enough dialogue. The characters don't express enough to each other, it is all very thin. Over the years I have developed a method where I write down what I want my characters to say and then compress that as much as possible into what they need to say. Herein lies the danger that in my eagerness I compress too much. I often do, which means that I am not giving the actors enough stages to get to the emotional point that they have to reach. I then have to go back and expand again, giving back those intermediate steps that I had so recklessly flung out.

I hold onto the script for as long as I can. I keep writing drafts and thinking of new things to try out. At last, when I can't delay any more, I hand it over to the director – who fortunately in my case has always been the same one so he knows what I mean and I trust what he does. I have nothing to do with casting and almost never have any particular actor or actress in mind when I am writing. I don't go on the set, there's nothing for me to do there. Sometimes I see rushes – just to see if things are working out the way we thought (they are usually different, but that is alright, they are supposed to be taking on a life of their own): and also to see if there are any scenes we could do without and thereby save money.

But there have been occasions when I see nothing until the rough cut. At that stage I begin to be very interested again. I go into the editing room and, together with the director and editor, fiddle around with what we have there. Here is another advantage of always being with the same director: we both know what the other is aiming for and it is usually the same thing. Mostly the film is much too long – I don't know why we never get this right – and so we have to decide how and where to cut. There are two criteria. One is that the story should move forward in the best (which is usually the clearest) way possible. The other is to throw out scenes that have not come out well and to retain those that have come out very well, even if they are not as strictly necessary to our purpose (the story and theme) as the former. There is some conflict of interest here, but in the end I think that the individual good scenes must win. One would simply not wish to discard something

CECIL
...Let me light your candle,
shall I.

He does so, carefully and gently, and gives it to her.

His voice is breaking as he speaks again.

CECIL
I must actually thank you for what
you've done - for your courage in
doing it. I do admire you for it.
Will you shake hands?

LUCY
Of course I will, Cecil.

They solemnly shake hands and then go out into the hall.

LUCY
Goodnight, Cecil. I'm sorry
about it. Thank you very much
for taking it so well.

94.   NIGHT.   INTERIOR.   PASSAGE AND STAIRS.

CECIL watches LUCY go upstairs, the shadows from the
banisters passing over her face like the beat of wings.

95.   NIGHT.   EXTERIOR.   GARDEN.

CECIL looks at Windy Corner as if he were saying goodbye.
He wanders about. He sees a figure glimmering in the dark
on the bench where he once proposed to LUCY. He
approaches -

CECIL
(surprised) Miss Bartlett?

He sits next to her.

CECIL
Aren't you going to bed?

CHARLOTTE
No, I like sitting here. I come
here quite often, after everyone's
asleep...Perhaps that surprises
you.

CECIL supports his head between his hands.

CECIL
Lucy has broken off our engagement.

2

CHARLOTTE says nothing.

CECIL
...If there were a reason - it
might be easier; even if there
were someone else -

CHARLOTTE
I hope you don't think that?

CECIL
Of course I don't. Of course
not, she didn't have to accuse
me of that.

A silence.

CECIL
Perhaps she is right, and I
can't love her as she should
be...loved; that I can't be
with anyone that way.

CHARLOTTE is looking up at the house which is quite dark
except for Lucy's window. LUCY's shadow can be seen
moving against it.

A silence. Perhaps they get up and walk about before he
starts up again.

CECIL
Perhaps I'm one of those who's
meant to live alone. Some of
us are...I think perhaps you are
too, Miss Bartlett.

CHARLOTTE
(after a pause) I dare say it
seems so now, but it wasn't always.
Not at all always. Certainly not
when I was Lucy's age...Look,
she's blown out her candle.

For the light in Lucy's window is extinguished, and
everything is dark.

TITLE CARD: LYING TO MR. BEEBEE, MRS. HONEYCHURCH, FREDDY
AND THE SERVANTS

96.   DAY.   INTERIOR.   BLOOMSBURY HOTEL BEDROOM-SITTING
ROOM

MISS CATHERINE ALAN is writing a letter to MR. BEEBEE,
sitting at a little writing table in a Spartan room. We

3

4

Jhabvala is always surprised by what she finds in the finished film and delighted when an actor has done something special on his own or a director has added a special touch. "For instance in **A Room With a View** after Lucy tells the priggish Cecil (1, 4) that she is not going to marry him, I wrote a rather boring dialogue scene between Cecil and Charlotte (Lucy's poor relative). It came out so awful that fortunately it was scrapped. Everything I tried to say in the dialogue was shown by Cecil sitting down and putting on his shoes very sadly. I didn't write that and it was wonderful." (2-3) The scene in the final draft.

Once you adapt a novel into a film, it is only the screenplay that matters, and getting it to work is the sole concern of the writer. Scenes will be radically altered and new ones will be invented. In **The Remains of the Day** Jhabvala felt that the housekeeper should have a life of her own, so she concocted a series of scenes for her and her husband (1–2). In **Howards End** there are no scenes in the novel between the two lovers to account for the birth of a baby, so Jhabvala wrote them in (3–5). In **A Room with a View** there is a question mark on George's plate which is not in the novel (6–8). Jhabvala wrote this in to suggest the questions whirling around in George's mind.

screenwriting

that is beautiful or interesting, or a wonderful bit of performance even if it is at a tangent to the main purpose. On the other hand, the main purpose has to be sacrificed if a scene is a failure. In **Howards End** one of the most crucial scenes is where the two sisters talk about their philosophy of life, which is to connect the different aspects of humanity. "Only connect!" is the entire motto and theme of the book! However, we had to ditch the scene where this is expressed because it was dull, and a dull scene equals disaster.

I always regard my sessions in the editing room as one more chance – the last – to improve the screenplay. It is magical to be able to switch scenes around, to contrast or correlate or counterpoint them with one another – even to change performances by eliminating tricks or devices actors have used unsuccessfully or excessively. It is amazing how one can do without certain steps that one thought at the time were absolutely essential for the story. For example in **The Golden Bowl**, we had a series of scenes where the Ververs decide to invite Charlotte to visit them – only to find in the editing room that we didn't need them; it was far more dramatic just to show the motor car with Charlotte inside it arriving at the door.

Quite frankly I feel that I have come to films from the wrong direction. They were never my prime interest, which was from the beginning literary. People who actually make films have a passion for them from a very young age. Not only did they see and were deeply impressed and influenced by films, they also learned about cameras and lighting and all the visual and technical stuff that to this day remain a mystery to me. I enjoy writing scripts but I know that I am doing no more than giving a blueprint for others to build from. Of course the blueprint is

essential and has to be worked out to the last possible detail – but I do not think that it has any value in itself. I don't find scripts interesting to read, it is as though they are waiting for something more, someone else to breathe life into them, as a composer breathes life into a libretto. This is one of the reasons why I do not like visiting a set. It's not only that there is nothing for me to do there – there isn't – but also that I am in the way: physically, insofar as I stumble over wires and have to be jostled aside by irritated crew members, but more seriously I am in the way of others doing their creative job of making the blueprint come alive. And in the process I don't want them to think of me at all – that is, of the script I've written. I want them to feel as free with the script as I was with the original novel. I love it when actors change the dialogue to make it fit them better, or add to it, or subtract, or reinterpret, or do whatever they wish to serve themselves. I want them to take possession of it for themselves, knowing that they will do so, much more than I could on the page, by infusing the words with their own talents and personalities.

And the same goes even more for the director, whose view or vision has to prevail over and transform the script. Often the chosen location offers unprecedented new angles – for instance, in **The Golden Bowl** the father delivers his warning to the errant son-in-law inside a huge and noisy steam engine which then acts as a sort of giant punctuation mark. And in **Mr. & Mrs. Bridge** so much is said of the relationship between husband and wife when in the Louvre the husband slyly glides his eye along the flank of a nude while at the same time aware of his wife innocently watching him. So while everyone is working on the set, what they are doing is transforming the script, transcending it. Yet the script has to be strong enough to bear such treatment – the basic

screenwriting

1

2

3

4

Jhabvala has a strong reputation for adaptations of classic novels including Kazuo Ishiguro's 'The Remains of the Day' (1), Henry James' 'The Bostonians' (2) and his 'The Golden Bowl' (3). (4) Ismail Merchant (left), Jhabvala and James Ivory (right), who make up the Merchant Ivory team, on location for **The Bostonians**.

the foundations and framework of a building, while the individual scenes must have an abundance of content in order to have every drop of meaning squeezed out of them.

I have very much enjoyed being involved in films and think of it as a great privilege that I owe to Merchant Ivory. However I do feel that, if I had not at the same time continued to write fiction, I would feel somewhat frustrated – because a film script is an unfinished thing, waiting to be brought into existence by the director and a whole team of artists and crew. If I had wanted the same creative fufilment that I have found in writing fiction, then I would have needed to direct the scripts I had written. But for that I know myself to lack every spark of the necessary talent, or interest – let alone the passion of those who are born and dedicated film-makers the way I regard myself as a born and dedicated novelist.

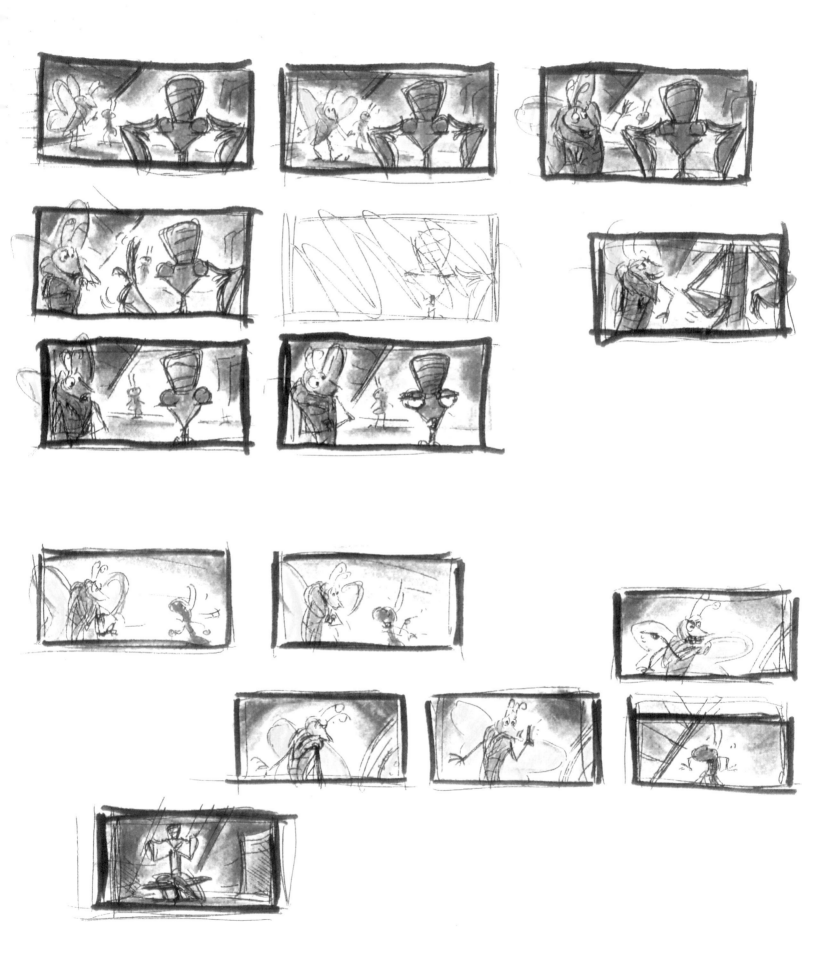

biography

Born in 1965 in Rockport, Massachusetts, the young Andrew Stanton used to enjoy filming short sketches on a Super-8 camera. During the summers, he worked as an usher in the small art-house theatre that a retired Hollywood producer ran in Rockport; there he would see foreign movies like **Diva** (Jean-Jacques Beineix, 1981), **Gallipoli** (Peter Weir, 1981) and **El Norte** (Gregory Nava, 1983) many times

andrew stanton

over. Although his main interest was acting, his talent for drawing drew him to animation, which he went on to study at the California Institute of the Arts (partially founded by Walt Disney). While at college, Stanton made short animated films, some of which were screened at festivals. At one festival during the '80s he met John Lasseter, the head of Pixar, a San Francisco company establishing a reputation for short animations. After college, Stanton worked as an artist with a large animation house in Los Angeles before receiving an offer to work with Lasseter on commercials. At first Stanton worked as an animator, but as Pixar were a small company he ended up getting involved in all parts of the production process, including writing. After two-and-a-half years, Lasseter was approached by Disney to make a feature. He kept the main team around him, including Stanton, who went on to write **Toy Story** (1995), **A Bug's Life** (1998), **Toy Story 2** (1999) and **Monsters, Inc.** (2002).

interview

If I did not have an insatiable desire to witness a new world full of living characters existing independently on a movie screen, I believe that all I would ever write is cheques. The thought of writing makes me groan with agony. The thought of drawing, animating, storyboarding or any other particular form of problem solving tires me out. Yet I have devoted most of my waking hours over the past 15 years to doing just this. It's because I love what the combination of all these storytelling steps produces – I love movies; I love watching them, I love analysing them. Most of all, I love making them.

When I started working with Pixar I was not a writer, but I very much knew what I wanted to see on the screen, and that is half the battle of screenwriting. At that time, animated feature films did not inspire me. None of them compared to a great non-animated movie. Animation may be unique as a visual medium, but from a storytelling standpoint I do not want to be judged differently from anybody else. I want to hold our films up against the best.

My generation, from Watergate-up, are cynical. We do not trust many institutions and we do not trust many people. We tend to think that there is a hidden agenda behind everything. The characters in animations of the '80s and early '90s did not reflect this darker attitude; when I began writing scripts, this was something I wanted to address. It is not that I want to make my characters cynical, because I am just as romantic, passionate and optimistic as any other storyteller would like to be. But I do desperately want the audience to relate with the characters in my story; only when that connection has been made will the audience be inspired by any romantic optimism in a script.

When I write, I am looking for that moment which contains such emotional resonance that it will carry the whole picture. This moment must be something universally "gettable". It must make you care so much that you will want to sit through the rest of the movie to see what happens. In **Toy Story** it was the visual image of the kid's favourite old toy (Woody) being knocked off his special spot on the bed, and a new modern toy (Buzz) being put there in his place. In **A Bug's Life** the moment is Flik messing up the harvest and putting his entire family in jeopardy. These events can potentially turn a character's world upside down. You may think up a million and one such moments, but it is hard to find the one that is universally gettable. We make family films that everyone is going to see; this forces us to make it gettable for both five-year-olds and studio executives, which is not a bad way of thinking. It is not that you want to dumb down. It is just that you want to communicate so clearly on an emotional level, not just on a plot level, that all people, even a kid who has not experienced life yet, are affected. You want to write the moment that will hit that primal part already wired into the child and wired into us. You are trying to tap into that jealousy, that fear, that greed or that whatever it is. It must be something resonant that ties into the plot, and also has major consequences for it.

This does not mean that I write for kids. Kids like anything. Kids don't have taste, they have to learn it. If you give them junk food they'll eat junk food. I want to give them stories that are as great as the stories in my favourite films. The consideration I'm going to give kids is to make sure I'm not excluding them by offending them, by introducing questionable morals or by writing something that they are not going to get at all and make them lose the story completely. Kids listen to adults talk all day about things they do not understand, but they get it by the tone of voice and the reactions. They use the same skills when watching a movie. They may not get what a character said, but if, for example, they see him punch the wall in frustration, then they will understand that emotional statement and be able to keep up with what's happening. Don't underestimate kids.

I work very differently from other screenwriters, because at Pixar I work as part of a group. Once we have the germ of an idea and need to expound upon it, I go off into a room and I am stuck with myself like every other writer. But I have the luxury of coming out of that room and having this group of guys who I trust with my creative life, to bounce ideas off and give me feedback to make the script better. If I had to write a serious drama or a very intense piece that was ultimately going to be depressing or scary, I could understand the idea of writing alone; it would make me more intense and introspective. However, on our scripts you're trying to capture wonder, fun and comedy, and that needs energy, life and

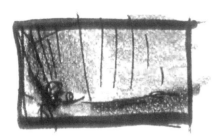

1

2

3

4

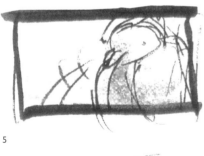

5

6

Francis and Dot fall into a crevice.

INT. CREVICE

It's a steep fall to the bottom. The sparrow lands above, causing tons of debris to rain down on them. A LARGE ROCK crashes onto Francis' leg, while a second knocks him unconscious.

EXT. EDGE OF ANT ISLAND

The Council members strain to see what's going on.

                    QUEEN/COUNCIL/ATTA
          I can't see...Somebody do
          something!...Are they alright?...Can
          anyone see?...Are they alive?...I can't
          see!...What is happening?!

Atta spies a dew drop on a nearby blade of grass.

EXT. BASE OF ANT ISLAND

Flik and the rest of the circus bugs scramble behind a boulder.

                    DOT (O.S.)
          Fliiik!

                    FLIK
          Dot?

They peer back at the dry riverbed. See the bird pecking furiously at the ground. Dot SCREAMS again.

                    MANNY
          Good heavens! They're in trouble!

                    SLIM
          Francis! Francis! Francis! Francis!...

                    FLIK
          Oh! Oh! You guys! I've got an idea!

EXT. EDGE OF ANT ISLAND

Atta pushes past the council, peering through the DEW-DROP TELESCOPE she's just made.

7

8

9

When developing a story for a film, Stanton will draw out thumbnail sketches, as in this scene from **A Bug's Life** (1–7). (8) Stanton in the Rockport art-house cinema (9) where he worked as a young man.

spontaneity. Having other people around reinforces and maintains that energy. It's especially important in our business, because the thing that kills animation is that it takes years to do.

I begin by writing a treatment of about 30 pages. Then I write a draft of the script, but we never consider that draft set in stone. It is simply a springboard to make the script visual. Before ever learning how to write a script, I made short animated films. I wrote them through drawing out storyboards. There was no written script. I went straight to the final image and saw what the characters told me to do. Nowadays I do write out a script, but I often get to a point where I think it

works and I want to road test it. Then I will start to thumbnail, which is drawing tiny storyboard images of the scene. During this process I often find some golden visuals springing from what seemed like a throwaway sentence in the script. Thumbnailing is my equivalent of doing a read-through with actors. It is often fascinating to see how much you can communicate without the word.

Once I have written something, I give it to the storyboard department who start drawing up visual representations (or "boards") of my script. When I think these visual representations are good enough, they get shot onto video and edited together to run like a movie. Then we watch a

(1) Flik from **A Bug's Life**. "We went in thinking that we had to do this very grand arc of Flik's character turning into something different. As I wrote it, I realised that it was about another dynamic. The main character didn't change, rather he changed the world of all the other characters in the story."

storyboard version of the script. It is all driven by economics because it is too expensive to animate and render the shots and then say it is no good. It is much cheaper (and takes minutes instead of days) to re-draw something. Viewing the storyboards run as a film on screen becomes part of the writing process. The text on the page is only one stage of the writing, yet it always ends up coming back to that text. It is like a flow chart going scriptwriting, storyboarding, onto the screen, doesn't work, back to the scriptwriting, storyboard and onto the screen. Depending on how close the deadline is or what the problem is, it may just go back to storyboarding, but in my mind storyboarding is still a form of writing or rewriting. All our movies are made through rewriting. Some

people think that rewriting is a horrible thing, but in my mind all scriptwriters rewrite in private until they decide that they have rewritten enough. The difference with me is that I invite the storyboarding and editorial departments into the writer's cabin during those early ugly rewrites that the writer would normally hide from everyone. If I sat there making my material perfect, without letting anyone touch it, this process would fall apart. It is a collaborative effort. The group is always there through the flow cycle to bounce ideas off. The script would also die if that group was stamping on every little stage of writing, because then it would end up being committee'd to death, but somehow we've miraculously found this great way of balancing it.

(1–20) "On **A Bug's Life**, to be realistic, the circus troupe had to comprise a number of characters. I had to decide which were the weaker characters and give them less lines. Writing for a lot of characters I sometimes felt like Mrs Partridge or Mrs Brady; busy changing diapers with one character and then suddenly realising that another character has been completely overlooked and has not had their share of time in the picture. You forgot they existed. The more characters you have, the more you have to be careful that you devote some screen time to each of them." (3–20) Sketches that helped Stanton develop a scene (1–2) featuring the circus troupe from **A Bug's Life**.

```
                    SLIM
          No, it's because I'm a PROP!  You
          always cast me as the broom, the
          pole, the stick, a SPLINTER --

                    P.T
          You're a walkingstick!  It's funny!
          NOW GO!!

                    SLIM
                 (walking out)
          You parasite.

Slim marches away, defiantly strapping a flower to his head.
The bug band strikes up a LYRICAL MELODY.

Two fireflies sit in the rafters above.  One shines his light
on the band.  He nudges his sleeping companion, who groggily
casts his light on the center ring.  The light falls on Slim
and Francis, dressed as a pair of flowers.

                    SLIM (CONT'D)
          Tra-la-la-la-la!  Spring is in the
          air, and I am a flower -- with
          nothing interesting to say.

                    FRANCIS
                 (looking backstage)
          Aaaah!

                    SLIM
          A bee!

                    FRANCIS
          Aaaah!

Heimlich, crudely dressed as a bee, inches out after the
other clowns.

                    HEIMLICH
          I am a cute little bumblebee!  Here
          I come.  (PANT) Slow down, you
          flowers!

The trio run past the stands where a small fly child is
holding onto a large candy corn.  Heimlich stops chasing the
other clowns and approaches the fly.

                    HEIMLICH (CONT'D)
          Oh!!  Candy corn!

Heimlichs'stomach GRUMBLES at the sight of food.

                    HEIMLICH (CONT'D)
                 (continued)
          Here, let me help you to finish it!
```

```
The fly boy defends his candy.

Francis, the ladybug, parades around the ring.  A PAIR OF
HECKLER FLIES ogle the ladybug.

                    HECKLER FLY #1
          Hey, cutie!  Wanna pollinate with a
          real bug?

The FLY elbows his buddy.  THEY BOTH LAUGH.

Francis daintily flies over to the Hecklers, smiling
demurely.

                    HECKLER FLY #1
          Ohhh, yeah!  Come to Poppa!

Francis reaches the flies, leans into Fly #1's face... and
explodes.

                    FRANCIS
                 (losing it)
          So being a ladybug automatically
          makes me a girl?!  Is that it,
          flyboy?!  Huh?!

                    HECKLER FLY #2
          Yikes!  She's a guy!

Slim and Heimlich suddenly notice what's going on.

                    HEIMLICH
          Francis, leave them alone!  They
          have poo-poo hands!

                    P.T. FLEA
          Not again.

P.T. pops backstage.

                    FRANCIS
          Judging by your breath, you musta
          'been buzzin'around a dung heap all
          day!

Slim and Heimlich are trying to pull Francis out of the
stands.

                    SLIM
          Come on, Francis.  You're making
          the maggots cry.

A MOTHER FLY sits one row up, holding TWO CRYING BABIES.
```

3

9

15

4

10

16

5

11

17

6

12

18

7

13

19

8

14

20

EXT. SID'S HOUSE - LATER THAT NIGHT

THUNDER RUMBLES as rain pours down outside the spooky
dwelling.

INT. SID'S ROOM

Sid is in bed fast asleep.

Woody struggle to move his milk crate jail, but with the
weight of the toolbox on top it won't budge.

Woody looks across the desktop at Buzz sitting dejectedly
with the rocket strapped to his back.

                    WOODY
          Ps-s-s-s-t! Psst! Hey, Buzz!

No reaction from Buzz.

Woody picks up a stray washer from the desktop and flings it
at Buzz, striking his helmet.

Buzz lifts his head and turns lifelessly to look at Woody.

                    WOODY (CONT'D)
          Hey! Get over here and see if you
          can get this tool box off me.

Buzz just looks away from Woody and bows his head.

                    WOODY (CONT'D)
          Oh, come on, Buzz. I... Buzz, I
          can't do this without you. I need
          your help.

                    BUZZ
          I can't help. I can't help anyone.

                    WOODY
          Why, sure you can, Buzz. You can
          get me out of here and then I'll
          get that rocket off you, and we'll
          make a break for Andy's house.

                    BUZZ
          Andy's house. Sid's house. What's
          the difference.

                    WOODY
          Oh, Buzz, you've had a big fall.
          You must not be thinking clearly.

                    BUZZ
          No, Woody, for the first time I am
          thinking clearly.
               (looking at himself)

2

                    BUZZ
          You were right all along. I'm not
          a Space Ranger. I'm just a toy. A
          stupid little insignificant toy.

                    WOODY
          Whoa, hey -- wait a minute. Being
          a toy is a lot better than being a
          Space Ranger.

                    BUZZ
          Yeah, right.

                    WOODY
          No, it is. Look, over in that
          house is a kid who thinks you are
          the greatest, and it's not because
          you're a Space Ranger, pal, it's
          because you're a TOY! You are HIS
          toy.

                    BUZZ
          But why would Andy want me?

                    WOODY
          Why would Andy want you?! Look at
          you! You're a Buzz Lightyear. Any
          other toy would give up his moving
          parts just to be you. You've got
          wings, you glow in the dark, you
          talk, your helmet does that -- that
          whoosh thing -- you are a COOL toy.

Woody pauses and looks at himself.

                    WOODY (CONT'D)
               (continued; depressed)
          As a matter of fact you're too
          cool. I mean -- I mean what chance
          does a toy like me have against a
          Buzz Lightyear action figure? All
          I can do is...

Woody pulls his own pull-string.

                    WOODY (VOICE BOX) (CONT'D)
          There's a snake in my boots!

Woody bows his head.

                    WOODY (CONT'D)
          Why would Andy ever want to play
          with me, when he's got you?
               (pause)
          I'm the one that should be strapped
          to that rocket.

3

Woody slumps dejectedly against the crate, his back to Buzz.

Buzz lifts up his foot.

ANGLE: THE SOLE OF BUZZ'S FOOT

The signature "ANDY" reads through the dirt and scuff marks.

Buzz gazes back at Woody. A look of determination spreads
across his face.

                    WOODY
          Listen, Buzz, forget about me. You
          should get out of here while you
          can.

Silence.

Woody turns around.

Buzz is gone.

Suddenly, the entire milk crate begins to shake. Woody looks
up to see...

                    BUZZ
          He is on top of the milk crate,
          trying to push the tool box off.

                    WOODY
          Buzz!! What are you doing? I
          thought you were --

                    BUZZ
          Come on, Sheriff. There's a kid
          over in that house who needs us.
          Now let's get you out of this
          thing.

                    WOODY
          Yes Sir!

Together, Buzz and Woody push the milk crate and get it to
move, but it's slow progress.

                    WOODY (CONT'D)
               (strained)
          Come on, Buzz! We can do it!

4

(2–4) Scene from **Toy Story** which develops the
relationship between Buzz and Woody (1).

Panel 1

[handwritten: SVLLEY BETTER IN SCHOOL THAN NED]

October 2, 1998
(A day that will live in infamy.)

[handwritten: PROFESSOR DISAPPOINTED WITH SULLIVAN AND DOING WELL IN SCHOOL (SUBCONSCIOUS EXPECTATION)]

Okay Everyone,

I didn't have as much time as I'd like to flesh out every moment; therefore, please forgive the occasional lengthy bland narrative. Unfortunately it doesn't read consistently like a treatment. Sorry, it was getting late. I decided to leave in certain annotations I make for myself when I write (**they're in bold**). I felt they would make some of my intentions for things a little clearer. Lastly, the Monster World can so easily become complicated and illogical that I made a list of rules for myself on how things run (society, scaring, etc...) Many of these details may never have to be addressed in the movie, but I wanted to have it all figured out, just in case. For your reading entertainment, I have included them.

Enjoy,

Andrew

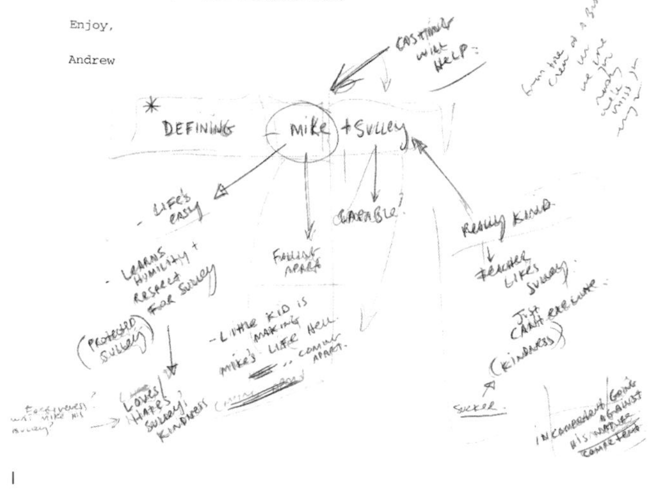

[handwritten diagram centered on circled "MIKE + SVLLEY" with "DEFINING" to the left and an asterisk; surrounding handwritten notes:]
CASTING WILL HELP
LIFE'S EASY
LEARNS HUMILITY + RESPECT FOR SVLLEY
(PROTECTED SVLLEY)
FALLING APART
LOVES/HATES SVLLEY'S KINDNESS
CAPABLE
REALLY KIND
TEACHER LIKES SVLLEY
JUST CAN'T EXPLAIN IT (KINDNESS)
LITTLE KID IS MAKING HELL IN MIKE'S LIFE - COMING APART
SUCKER
INCONGRUENT/GOING AGAINST HIS NATURE - COUNTERS

1

Panel 2

the back of the photo is the apartment number (or building
**address) of her friends. This could be what Mike uses to get help
in Act 3.**

As the two monsters attempt to communicate with Boo, we cut
to her POV. The monsters voices sound deep, gurgled, and
unintelligible. Boo is unable to understand them.

The monsters on the other hand, have all taken their proper
language courses (at least Sullivan), and she doesn't seem to be
speaking any language they've heard of.

The little girl keeps pointing at Mike an saying the words
"Oo! Wee leppy karn!"

**Show that Boo is very adversarial here. At her meanest, most
like a ferocious little animal.**

•Next Morning.

Mike returns with picnic basket and borrowed car **(who did he
borrow it from?).**

While Mike was gone, Sullivan has bonded a bit with the girl.
Turns out that Sullivan is natural with children. He's figured
out what she likes to eat. Taken her potty (after one unfortunate
accident) and has even given her a name: "Boo". Seems that
whenever he tries to scare her, yelling the word "Boo!", the girl
just laughs and laughs.

Sullivan has found an opening with Boo, but it is not
consistent. **She should still be unpredictable.** Just when they
think they've tamed her, she bites back.

•Plan "A" - "Ditch Her".

While driving to the outskirts of town **(the woods?)**, Sullivan
is having second thoughts about how they plan to get rid of Boo.
Mike is unmoved: "Do you want to be banished?" "Of course not."
"Do want to ever get a chance to scare, Mr. I was born to scare?"
"Yes." "Then we ditch her."

•Try To Ditch Boo.

****What do Mike and Sullivan do that distracts Boo, allowing
them to run to the car and drive away.**

Keep Boo disagreeable, bordering on unlikable, but right when

MI Treatment (9/98)   Pg.6

2

Panel 3

it's time to drive off she gets cute on them. **(How?)**

The two monsters drive some distance before Mike finally
gives under the pressure from Sullivan to turn around.

Show that Boo is pretty stubborn. She won't let either of
the monsters touch her. Very independent. Unwilling to accept
that she needs help in doing anything. Still she's just so damn
cute. Instill image of her not willing to take Sullivan's hand
back into the car. Will do it herself.

•Out Of Gas.

When the car doesn't start, Mike blames Sullivan making them
turn around, using up the gas.

Boo's giggles and laughs get them back.

Overlap Dialogue to go to...

•Disguise Boo.

... their apartment where Sullivan is rummaging through the
closet for material to disguise Boo as a monster. They discuss
"Plan B": disguise Boo as a monster, bring her to MI, have Mike
request her door, and send Boo back home. Mike and Sullivan argue
over how Boo's disguise should look, both unconsciously wanting
her to resemble themselves. While busy arguing, Boo has made her
own disguise and manages to scare both Mike and Sullivan. Guess
it will do.

Again Boo is a little more relaxed, but still volatile.

•Plan "B" - Get the door.

Sullivan goes to Linguist department.

Henry Higgins type monster.

*Set up Ireland Solution here somehow.

***What is Sullivan's excuse for bringing an non-English
speaking child monster to the MI language department?**

Mike looks up door number in register. Simultaneously, S & M
discover that Boo is from Ireland. Dingle County exactly. This
explains her thick Gaelic inflected Irish accent.

Mike Tries to get Door. Showing the golden rod colored
receipt that Sullivan kept. Clerk justs laughs at Mike, "Who died
and made you boss?" Sorry. Assigned to Ned. Only Ned, or if
sick, his understudy, can get door.

Mike is about to leave when he turns to ask where the door is

[handwritten margin notes alongside: various including "GAELIC"]

MI Treatment (9/98)   Pg.7

3

Panel 4

from. - cut to "Ireland?!" Or. Sullivan wrote the number down
and checks it against the big globe. Each door has an exact
longitude and latitude.

Boo gets away from Sullivan and into the Shredder. **Maybe
things were going really well with the two until Sullivan DID
WHAT?**

[handwritten: See - 2ND SHREDDER NEED SET-UP]

•Rescue Boo.

Sullivan gets Boo just in time, but cameras detects Boo. Her
disguise is eaten by the shredder, but Boo manages to escape it.
Cameras detect her presence and the "child infestation" alarm goes
off. Boo might even be mad at Sullivan. Maybe she wanted
something from the shredder. A little dollie or something
attractive. She had no idea she was about to be shredded. All
she knows is that Sullivan grabbed her before she could get the
dollie. (backpack?) Maybe Sullivan was holding on to it OR when
he looks away for a second, he turns back to see only her
backpack. **She took it off so she could fit through some vent or
opening to get to dollie.**

•Lockdown!

Sullivan and Boo get out in time, but Mike is caught in lock
down. Karen Silkwood moment. Meet in the parking lot. Mike is
all puffy and funny looking. Again, Boo points laughs while
saying "wee leppy karn." Sullivan realizes that she's been
calling Mike a leprauchan and can't help but laugh himself. Mike
is not amused. Sullivan, "Did you get the door?" Mike: "No."
Sullivan: "Then what are we gonna do?" Mike smirks, "Ned is going
to be out sick Monday."

**When we're out in the parking lot, Boo is berating Sullivan
still denying her the dollie. Sullivan is trying to keep her
quiet. When they see Mike, they both crack up (bond moment).**

•Plan "C" - Get Ned Sick

Remembering that Ned hates bananas, the trio shadow Ned all
weekend and attempt to slip a banana into his diet. Time after
time they try, but always failing. **Use Boo directly because he
doesn't recognize her?** Finally they throw away their last banana
in frustration. Ned slips on the peel, down a flight of stairs,

MI Treatment (9/98)   Pg.8

4

(1-4) "These pages are from an early treatment of **Monsters, Inc.** The
bold type shows changes from the previous draft and indicates plot and
character issues that needed resolving."

A script should have a momentum, like a piece of music. Once you find that you want to keep it going. You strive in the script stage to see how much of a page-turner you can make it, and once you get it up in a rough form on storyboards (reels) and watch it like a movie, you look for the lulls when you're ready to go for popcorn. The minute something seems to be lagging, the minute you don't care, the minute you don't want to turn the page we stop, analyse and ask, "Why did that happen?" Nine times out of ten, the problem is not at the point where your interest lagged; it is something earlier that was not set up correctly, either information you did not get across or an emotion that you assumed people would have. Much rewriting is driven by that fundamental lag.

I've heard writers say, "I don't write films for anybody else but myself". That only works if you are writing for the part of you that goes out after work just wanting to be entertained. It is true that I only know how to write a movie that I would like. But I do not want to write a movie that I alone would like; I want to write it for someone that just loves going to the movies, and that to me is not selfish, it is very selfless. People lead busy lives and their time is valuable. If they go to a movie that I have written I want them to feel that it was worth it. I know how grateful I feel when I have been transported somewhere for two hours. You sit through 6,000 movies that you hate in the hope that you will find another one that will transport you away. Economically, we are in the business of writing blockbuster films. That does not necessarily mean it has to be a certain type of story. It does mean that it should consume and involve the audience.

When I first started writing, I took the term, "it's all in the ending", to mean you should end with a big spectacle like a car chase; but it really refers to the emotional payoff when all these highs and lows and twists and turns come to a summation. I realised that the inspiration for a movie can be derived from anything, but inspiration to actually make a movie should ideally come from an idea for an ending.

We discovered our ending for **Toy Story** by complete accident. We thought it was our beginning: what if a toy was left behind at a rest stop? How would that feel? How would it feel as a child to know that toy was looking for you as hard as you were looking for it? This simple scene quickly conjured up emphatic feelings in all of us. It was universally gettable. However, this idea became our ending and not our beginning. Buzz and Woody do get physically lost in the movie, and are trying to get home throughout the film, but the emotional aspiration to "get back home" was not cemented and truly executed until the end. Everything in the climax was about that simple rest stop idea: my family is driving away, and if I miss that ride I will lose them forever. I'm so desperate to catch up that I will do everything in my power to get home. Add to that the willingness to sacrifice yourself so your friend will get home instead of you, and you have got powerful stuff.

The film ends with Buzz and Woody chasing after a moving van to get back home. They have to get into that van, but their batteries go and it looks like they will not make it. The script was written so that Woody has one match that he uses to light a rocket; this rocket saves the day by propelling them into the van. We watched it and realised that the movie-going audience, being very savvy on how movies work, will identify that one match and know instantly that we are going to use it to save our heroes. At this point, the movie was almost done, but we thought, what if he lights the match as before, but a

1

car goes over it and puts out the flame? And we all went, "That's great! They're screwed!" We loved how that would feel watching the film, but we had no clue how the hell to get our heroes out of that problem; but it is for such moments that we go to the cinema, so we were determined to find our way out of this story knot. We looked back at the earlier part of the movie and found a bit where Sid burns a little hole on Woody's forehead with a magnifying glass and realised that same magnifying glass effect could be used to start the flame. Woody would recall the incident and use it. Right in the middle of putting together this new ending some technical guys informed us that Buzz's plastic helmet could never truly magnify the sun; but we knew it wouldn't matter. At that point, people are so satisfied that you blew out the match and gave them such a great movie moment that they will let it go. We took the gamble and it worked. That moment was written purely by staying in tune with the part of you that loves going to the movies.

(1) "**Monsters, Inc.** was about a completely made-up world. The artists came up with the fantastical look, but the difficult bit was giving that world its own rules. In another story that would have been worrying about the frosting before making the cake. On a fantasy movie like **Monsters, Inc.** it was fundamental to know what the playground was before letting your characters run around in it. The audience will accept your rules, regardless of how weird they are. A Grimm's fairy tale can start, 'There was a sausage and a mouse and a bird and they lived in a house together', and amazingly you accept that sausages, birds and mice can live together, but the storyteller must be consistent with that rule. One of the biggest weaknesses in fantasy movies is when problems are just solved by unexplained magic. If that can happen, why should the audience care?"

biography

In 1945 Krzysztof Piesiewicz was born into a Warsaw that had just been flattened by the Germans. The destruction in Poland was retribution for the Warsaw uprising against the Nazis, an uprising in which Piesiewicz' own father had fought. As a baby Piesiewicz breathed in air filled with dust from the rubble which remained after the destruction, and as a result, along with many others, suffered from the "ruins illness". 25

krzysztof piesiewicz

years later he graduated from the Faculty of Law at Warsaw University. After martial law was declared in Poland in December 1981, he became a defence counsel for the Solidarity Trade Union in numerous political trials. When the pro-Solidarity priest Father Jerzy Popieluszko was murdered by security policemen, Piesiewicz was the assistant prosecuting counsel in the case against his killers. In 1982 Piesiewicz met the film-maker, Krzysztof Kieslowski, who was trying to make a documentary about the political trials. Piesiewicz wrote 18 screenplays with Kieslowski, including **Dekalog** (1988), **The Double Life of Véronique (La Double Vie de Véronique**, 1991), and the **Three Colours** trilogy (**Trois Couleurs**, 1993–94). Shortly before Kieslowski's death, they wrote a short story treatment entitled 'Heaven' which was the basis of the first part of another trilogy: **Heaven** (Tom Tykwer, 2002), 'Hell' and 'Purgatory'. Piesiewicz completed these scripts and continues to write in between his work for the Polish Senate, where he has represented Warsaw since the establishment of a democracy in Poland in 1989.

interview

Most modern scripts appear to be written about something the writer has seen in a newspaper or on TV. Every day dozens of such usable stories may appear; but that is not a reason to spend the large amounts of time, effort and money needed to make them into a film. If I want to explore a theme, loneliness for example, I will not take some relevant newspaper anecdote and then develop it into a script. Instead, I look for those protagonists that best express my idea. I do not know how I pick these characters, maybe it is by intuition. They could be young or old, male or female, but once I have found them I will live with them and spend time with them. Only then can I know what they will do. As I write the script I will never assume or foresee what will happen to my characters. Rather, I write it scene by scene as if I myself am living this life. Only then will it be credible.

When I was a young barrister, I found the crime far less interesting than why the person committed it. My professor in law school taught us that the good lawyer must imagine the situation in which the criminal finds himself. A good judge must put himself in the shoes of the thief, feeling the emotions and passions the thief felt. So the writer must do the same with his characters.

When I was a small child, it was a time of official lies in Poland. The story of Poland had been changed in schoolbooks, so I learnt my history from books at home. There was censorship, but at least everyone knew it was there. Films were made and books were written according to the censor's rules, but most artists looked for ways to bypass the censor using subtle means. This clash between censorship and rebellion produced very interesting results. During totalitarianism, the two most successful means of anti-establishment expression were music and poetry. In cinema, screenwriters avoided political and social subjects and dealt more with emotional ones. That is why there are so many beautiful films from Poland at this time pertaining to everyday humane and psychological problems.

Indeed in Poland in the '70s, we had the "cinema of moral anxiety", which came out of a feeling that the world as it really existed was not being depicted – particularly for us Poles who lived under this communist censorship. I think this style of cinema, in some small way, contributed to the explosion of the Solidarity Trade Union movement which changed the state, because it allowed people to better understand the world around them. It showed us that we had something in common and that we could do things together.

Kieslowski and I did write about the political trials in the film **No End**, but after it was made we were attacked from all angles. The regime thought it promoted the opposition, while the opposition had wanted it to be a propaganda movie for the

resistance. Meanwhile the Church criticised the morals in the movie. So after **No End**, we felt that we had to stay clear of politics and deal with the moods of individuals. We felt that the sum of these individuals would illustrate the life of the community. We did this through a series of ten films based on the Ten Commandments. Called **Dekalog**, they portray the daily simple life of that time. It was a world without banality; when everything functioned within a cold social realism. This cold realism in turn triggered a hunger for the absolute, for spirituality and the metaphysical. During martial law people found shelter in the Church, both physically and intellectually but also spiritually. This raised an interesting question – was this need for the Church born out of ritual or a real longing for the absolute? This question was explored in the scripts.

After years of Nazi and Stalinist totalitarianism, Poland is now a democracy thanks to the heroes of the Warsaw uprising and Solidarity movement. Unfortunately in this free space of today, the arts have become less intensive, less true and more shoddy. When communism fell, I thought that we would defend ourselves against the shoddiness of the mass-media tabloid culture; however, every year we are flooded with more of it. Although we created democracy in Poland, we didn't manage to bring back the moods and thinking that we had in August 1980 when Solidarity was established. Then the workers on strike were reading the poetry of [Czeslaw] Milosz. During the Solidarity era, as a barrister, I defended bus drivers in Warsaw who printed underground uncensored poetry. How is it possible that the same people, who in the past printed such poetry, today sit in front of their TV sets and watch idiotic programmes? I cannot understand it. Now, more and more people view the world as it is shown on TV,

(1) 'The Taking of Christ' by Michelangelo Caravaggio. "Once when I was in Rome I went to see a Caravaggio picure in a darkened church, and I had to put a coin into this special machine to make the light come on. Suddenly, the picture appeared in an incredible play of colours and it felt as if I was at the cinema. I feel that modern films should be like a Caravaggio picture, with everything supposedly realistic but some small details giving it a mysterious and spiritual dimension." (2–3) Photographs from the Warsaw Ghetto, which was destroyed by the Nazis as retribution for the Polish uprising. "I'm very attached to Warsaw. It is a symbol of what brutality can lead to. I think it is important today not to just show pictures of the concentration camps and Warsaw in ruins, as they could be perceived as mere postcards from the past. We must show the mechanisms that create such atrocities because they happen in very normal situations. As trains in Warsaw were transporting people to Auschwitz, restaurants were open and filled with people chatting and drinking coffee, doing what people like to do in every city."

screenwriting

Stills from **Three Colours: Red** (1) and **Three Colours: White** (3). (2) Piesiewicz (fourth from right) at the Cannes screening of **Three Colours: Red**.

perceiving themselves through the people on the TV rather than seeing the situations that they really live in. This is terribly strange. Now, as a writer, when you try to show something beyond just physical activity, more and more of the audience do not understand what you are trying to achieve. Unfortunately, this is a worsening trend.

Research shows that 90 per cent of people's knowledge now comes via the moving image in all its forms. Today there are hundreds of thousands of people with cameras who describe the world for us and send their pictures all over the planet. Perhaps the symbol of the 20th century should be the photograph, since the 20th century has been documented in images like no other. However, there is a limit to what news and documentary can achieve. I believe that the feature film will become more and more noble as a response to this proliferation of the filmed image. It will deal with problems that the news and documentary films are not able to show us about motivation, about dreams, about happiness, about hatred, about everything that is not visible. Although we now have so much TV news and many documentaries, we don't know anything more about the world. We don't know how people feel, their attitude towards other people, what they want, what pain they experience, what they are missing and what motivates their behaviour. We have the news from Shanghai, New York and Argentina, but we often do not understand the people that pass us by on the street.

A writer should train to be perceptive and develop the ability to stop and focus on the world around him. A scriptwriter must also become trained in the language of film. Cinema should not be about dialogue. A scriptwriter who tries to render the nature of the script solely through the dialogue will

fail. The scriptwriter needs to use words in a way that makes the reader see pictures first, rather than emotions. The words should form sentences, and these sentences should turn into pictures that express emotion. This is the art of scriptwriting. It takes great skill to describe in words the pictures that exemplify pain, joy, despair, hopelessness and love. It is difficult but not impossible – you can learn a lot by looking at the paintings of the great artists.

The contemporary scriptwriter must now also understand how much he can condense a story. Kieslowski and I used to joke about what we called "Bulgarian Cinema" of the '60s and '70s. Characters in Bulgarian films would be shown performing every action very precisely; for example, getting into the bath and getting out of the bath or going out onto the balcony and coming back from the balcony. Nowadays commercials and pop promos have prepared young viewers for a greater synthesis of storytelling. This is progress. For a long time, we had big films that were the cinematic equivalent of the books of Balzac or Dickens. I think that **The Godfather** marked the end of this epoch. Now cinema has developed a new autonomous means of expression and it is evolving as literature did; it has become more like poetry than prose, and good modern cinema shall raise the questions which were asked by great literature. Paradoxically, this new cinematic language is being created in the world of commercials.

In my scripts there is always a subject I want to discuss with the viewer. I start by asking myself whether this subject is significant, and whether I have anything to say about it. The actual subjects or themes arise from my own introspection. Once I have my subject or theme, I start and write the first scene while being aware of what I shall say in the last scene.

                    PAWEL
If...someone Died abroad, would
there be an announcement as well?

                    KRZYSZTOF
If someone was prepared to pay for
it.

                    PAWEL
Dad..

Something in Pawel's voice makes Krzysztof put down the
newspaper.

                    PAWEL (CONT'D)
Why do people die?

                    KRZYSZTOF
It varies. Sometimes because of
heart attacks, or accidents, or old
age..

                    PAWEL
No, I mean, why do people have to
die at all?

                    KRZYSZTOF
See what it says under 'death' in
the encyclopaedia.

Pawel gets up and takes down the relevant volume from a shelf
crammed full of various kinds of encyclopaedias. He flicks
through the pages, evidently accustomed to looking things up
in it, and reads aloud.

                    PAWEL
'..a phenomenon caused by the
irreversible cessation of all the
functions of the bodily organism,
the heart, the central nervous
system..' What's the central
nervous system?

                    KRZYSZTOF
Look it up - there's an entry under
the heading.

                    PAWEL
It didn't have anything.

                    KRZYSZTOF
It must have. It's got everything
that can be described and
understood. Man is a machine. The
heart is like a pump and the brain
is like a computer.

4

5

6

7

                    KRZYSZTOF (CONT'D)
They get exhausted and then stop
working - that's all there is to
it. What's up. Is something wrong?

                    PAWEL
Nothing..only..

Pawel point to the newspaper.

                    PAWEL (CONT'D)
..they say something here about 'a
service for the peace of her soul'.
There's nothing about the soul in
the encyclopaedia.

                    KRZYSZTOF
It's just a term. It doesn't really
exist.

                    PAWEL
Antie thinks it does.

                    KRZYSZTOF
Some people find it easier to cope
with life if they think it does.

                    PAWEL
Do you?

                    KRZYSZTOF
Me? No. Is anything the matter?

                    PAWEL
No, nothing.

                    KRZYSZTOF
Well?

                    PAWEL
I saw a dead dog today. As I was
coming back with the papers. The
one with the yellow eyes. It was
always cold and hungry and hung
around the dustbins. Know the one I
mean?

                    KRZYSZTOF
Yes.

                    PAWEL
Right. Well I was so pleased I got
the answer right this morning....and
it was just lying there and it's
eyes were completely glazed over.

(1) This 15th-century picture from the Warsaw
Museum, portraying the Ten Commandments
in a contemporary setting, inspired Piesiewicz
with the idea for the **Dekalog**. "I spent hours
looking at this picture because from it I could
learn about the times when the artist painted
it." (2–7) A scene from **Dekalog 1**, where the
young Pawel questions his father on the
meaning of death.

2

3

The themes I dealt with in the **Three Colours** trilogy were the ideals of the French Revolution: liberty, equality and fraternity, as represented in the blue, white and red of the French *tricolore*. The trilogy was developed in 1989 while the Berlin Wall was being pulled down. At the time, I felt that these slogans would reappear in our world. I also had personal experience of how these ideals functioned in Poland. People do not really want liberty or freedom. They want the freedom to make decisions, but in reality these decisions will turn them into slaves overnight. For example, people "freely" decide to work hard to make money; but this decision is simply something which materialism is demanding of them. Working hard, they then become totally dependant on this materialism because they expect it to be a way of escaping loneliness. Finally, they realise it is a trap. Equality is a beautiful idea used by totalitarian systems to create conformity and destroy our acceptance of anything that is different. Fraternity is effectively love, but love has now become more difficult to find. However, it is fraternity that can rescue you. Without fraternity the other two slogans are very dangerous indeed, as my own country has experienced. When faced with such slogans, remember that there are certain basic notions that must not be sacrificed for any ideal. When Stalin and Hitler ruled Poland, they used to say that they were doing it for my benefit. The most dangerous colleagues of mine in the Parliament are those who ply the notion of the general "good". There is no general "good", there is only the individual happiness of people in their own personal worlds.

The "Heaven", "Hell" and "Purgatory" trilogy of scripts make up another description of reality using three notions that exist in our society. I was born in the Warsaw ruins, right after the Nazi occupation, and I constantly heard people talking about the dreadful events in the concentration camps where they had lost loved ones. The people among whom I was brought up had to fight, kill and commit terrible acts so that others would not be killed. These people were still beautiful because, in spite of these dreadful experiences, they had paradise within them. Today I know people who have everything yet they want to antagonise and manipulate others. These people have hell inside them. Most people have purgatory inside them. Possibly, these are the most interesting individuals from the scriptwriting point of view because they show that people have a conscience. Starting with these fundamental ideas, I found characters and through them constructed the stories that explored my ideas of heaven, hell and purgatory.

While I believe that a writer must begin by asking himself what it is that he wants to say, the writer should never have a mission. Somebody who has a mission very quickly becomes an ideologist; in this case an ideologist with a computer or a camera. Many writers in Poland were ideologists wanting to persuade their public that there is only one way to see the world. The artist should kindly and truly describe the human world. Nothing more. For myself, I would not like to teach morals to anyone. That is not my speciality. As a writer, I follow my intuition and my everyday experience. I will continue to put words into sentences and sentences into pictures as long as my shrewdness does not become feeble, and as long as I can recognise those questions that people have, but are often afraid to raise in public. It is difficult to know when one can no longer do such things, so now I ask young people and my own children whether I can still see and understand what is going on.

1

2

4

3

5

(1–5) Stills and posters from the **Three Colours** trilogy. "I'm not sure how I pick the characters that best illustrate the ideas that I want to explore. Perhaps it is by intuition. Most often they are women, as women give you more possibilities of expression. They are more spontaneous and more beautiful than men, but at the same time they can be quite cruel and calculating. After all, their influence extends into every aspect of life."

(1) Piesiewicz with Kieslowski. "I try not to talk about my working relationship with Kieslowski. All I can tell is what he used to say; that the main ideas, since the moment we met, came from me – but let the rest be kept between the two of us." (2) Kieslowski and Irene Jacob in **The Double Life of Véronique**. "I don't like to talk about the events in these films, because everyone should interpret them for themselves. You know the kind of question you ask a pupil in school, 'What did the author or the poet want to express in this poem?' I try to avoid any possibility of being judged or experienced in this way." Stills from (3) **A Short Film about Love**, and (5) **Dekalog** 1. (4) Poster for **A Short Film about Killing**. Piesiewicz' script told a story very close to his own experience – that of a young defence lawyer involved in a brutal murder case.

4

5

A very wise professor once told me how he was brought up in a beautiful palace as part of a very rich aristocratic family. Then when the Second World War was over he lost it all and all he was left with was one pair of torn trousers and shoes with holes. He began to study the history of religion and went on to become one of the most astounding experts in the world in his field and befriended Professor Wojtyla, who later became Pope. If instead he had gone on living cheerfully and comfortably in his palace, he would never have achieved so much, met so many interesting people, written so many books, and at the end of his life he would not be so happy. He told me that real creativity must take place in an ascetic environment. You don't have to be hungry or give up a comfortable flat, but you do have to give up other temptations such as an easy career, shoddiness and glitter. You must observe the world and speak the truth. To choose honesty and truth is the small heroism of the artist.

biography

When Francis Ford Coppola accepted his screenwriting Oscar for **The Godfather** in 1972 he thanked Robert Towne for his contribution to the script. Ever since 1967, when Warren Beatty hired him to do some rewriting on **Bonnie and Clyde** (Arthur Penn), Towne had developed a reputation as one of Hollywood's top script doctors. Born in Los Angeles in 1934, Towne was raised in San Pedro, California. The young Towne

robert towne

always wanted to write, although he thought he would have become a journalist. He was asked to write his first screenplay by producer/director Roger Corman, whom he had met at an acting class. The screenplay was called 'The Tomb of Ligeia' (1964). In 1973 Towne picked up his own Oscar for Best Adapted Screenplay with **The Last Detail** (Hal Ashby); the following year he won the Academy Award for Best Original Screenplay with **Chinatown** (Roman Polanski). Towne collaborated with Beatty to write **Shampoo** (Hal Ashby, 1975) and **Reds** (Warren Beatty, 1981), before writing and directing **Personal Best** (1982). Unhappy with changes to his script for **Greystoke: The Legend of Tarzan** (Hugh Hudson, 1984), Towne replaced his credit with the name of his dog, P. H. Vazak. Vazak was nominated for an Oscar. Towne's other writing credits include **The Two Jakes** (Jack Nicholson, 1990), **Days of Thunder** (Tony Scott, 1990), **The Firm** (Sydney Pollack, 1993) and **Mission: Impossible II** (John Woo, 2000). In 1997 he was presented with the Writers Guild Screen Laurel Award for lifetime contributions to the art of screenwriting.

interview

My training as a writer began in an acting class. Acting is actually a great apprenticeship for writing because you get a feeling for language. You also quickly learn that the actual words people use are not nearly as important as the intent behind them. In that class I would improvise, and watch people like Jack Nicholson improvising several times a week for seven or eight years. We were given situations as basic as this: there are two of you and you know the other will die if she goes through a certain door. You must stop her from going through that door, but you are not allowed to mention either death or the door. Through improvising situations like these, you learn to communicate something without directly mentioning it. This is important in all forms of dramatic writing, because people usually say one thing and mean another. This applies to screenwriting more than any other form, because the picture conveys so much information that it is almost impossible for dialogue to add to it. On the stage, there is not as much visual language, so the dialogue must carry more information. But in a movie you see more and you see it quicker. Therefore what you hear has to be different

from what you see. An awful lot of screenwriting is figuring out what not to say.

On daytime TV, when the characters talk, what you see is what you get. They sound unbelievably real and yet the programmes make you feel bored and depressed. This is because there is no compression or distillation of events. In a good movie, although everything including the dialogue seems utterly realistic, every scene is a compression of experience. One scene represents ten scenes. Good screenwriters create plenty of subtext by stacking and heightening experience in this way.

Although nobody is ever going to see it, the only way to be sure of distilling something is to overwrite it as if you had all the time in the world to explore the scene. That way you're not going to leave out anything vital. My tendency now is to write longer and longer scenes. Instead of a 150-page draft, I'm doing a 350-page draft. When I go to compress that draft it will paradoxically be easier to do because I have made it as full as it can be. I am less likely to leave out something essential from the final draft because it is already there in the initial one. The scene, for example, in **The Firm** between the two Morolto brothers at the end (which doesn't feature in the book), was originally written with 17 pages. In the final screenplay it had been edited down to four.

When you start writing a script your goal is to take yourself out of the equation as quickly as possible. It's like a dance; you start off leading in the hope that you will be following as soon as possible. If you are the one pushing the story for too long, there is something wrong. Whereas if the story starts dictating the direction it is going, then something is right. Good writing must be coming from within your characters. The whole point is to isolate and identify with what a character wants and what a character fears. Then work out how that character reacts to those wants and fears. If there is a disparity between where I think the screenplay is going to go and where the characters seem to dictate that it goes, then I go with the characters and make the adjustments accordingly. You want to go with the behaviour that you think is most truthful.

Reading J. D. Salinger taught me that people generally (and perhaps Americans particularly) do not use dialogue with nearly as much precision as would seem from the dialogue you read in many books and scripts. Salinger made me realise that some of the most eloquent statements are made when people cannot quite say something the way they mean. In **Shampoo**, the hairdresser George is asked how he is, and he replies, "I'm cutting too much hair and losing all my concepts". Nobody really knows what that means, but in a strange way you get a very good idea of the true meaning of his statement. The audience knows that George is in a rat race and wants to take a step back and get some control over his life, rather than get lost in one lady's head of hair after another (and their lives and their bodies and everything else). Viewed within that context, the line, "I'm cutting too much hair and losing all my concepts", becomes oddly clear and so much better than him saying, "I feel molested and alienated".

The main character in Salinger's "The Catcher in the Rye", Holden Caulfield, recognises that some things are almost too important to try and be too articulate about. He is unwilling to be too specific when communicating because he's aware that

2

3

4

5

6

"I don't know how I came to write **Chinatown**, although I can point to individual steps along the way; I saw a series of photographs by John Waggaman in *West* magazine (3–6), appended to an article called 'Raymond Chandler's Los Angeles'. The photographs really affected me; they reminded me of the city that I grew up in. I was suddenly filled with a tremendous kind of sense of loss, of what that city once was. And you could see the little pockets of time that could throw you right back into the past. And I knew that it was still possible to photograph the city in such a way as to recreate that time, much in the way that those street lamps existed. And I suppose, in a way, that was the beginning." Towne (1) and with the young Jack Nicholson (2), whom he met at acting school.

225   Gittes pushes past him. Evelyn, looking a little worn but glad to see him hurries to the door. She takes Gittes' arm.

                 EVELYN
      How are you? I was calling you.

She looks at him, searching his face.

                 GITTES
      -- Yeah?

They move into the living room. Gittes is looking around it.

                 EVELYN
      Did you get some sleep?

                 GITTES
      Sure.

                 EVELYN
      Did you have lunch? Kyo will fix
      you something --

                 GITTES
          (abruptly)
      -- where's the girl?

                 EVELYN
      Upstairs. Why?

                 GITTES
      I want to see her.

                 EVELYN
      ... she's having a bath now... why
      do you want to see her?

Gittes continues to look around. He sees clothes laid out for packing in a bedroom off the living room.

                 GITTES
      Going somewhere?

                 EVELYN
      Yes, we've got a 4:30 train to
      catch. Why?

Gittes doesn't answer. He goes to the phone and dials.

                 GITTES
      -- J. J. Gittes for Lieutenant
      Escobar...

                    (CONTINUED)

1

---

225   CONTINUED:

                 EVELYN
      What are you doing? What's wrong?
      I told you we've got a 4:30 --

                 GITTES
          (cutting her off)
      You're going to miss your train!
          (then, into phone)
      ... Lou, meet me at 1412 Adelaide
      Drive -- it's above Santa Monica
      Canyon... yeah, soon as you can.

                 EVELYN
      What did you do that for?

                 GITTES
          (a moment, then)
      You know any good criminal lawyers?

                 EVELYN
          (puzzled)
      -- no...

                 GITTES
      Don't worry -- I can recommend a
      couple. They're expensive but you
      can afford it.

                 EVELYN
          (evenly but with
           great anger)
      What the hell is this all about?

Gittes looks at her -- then takes the handkerchief out of his breast pocket -- unfolds it on a coffee table, revealing the bifocal glasses, one lens still intact. Evelyn stares dumbly at them.

                 GITTES
      I found these in your backyard --
      in your fish pond. They belonged to
      your husband, didn't they?... didn't
      they?

                 EVELYN
      I don't know. I mean yes, probably.

                 GITTES
      -- yes positively. That's where
      he was drowned...

                 EVELYN
      What are you saying?

                    (CONTINUED)

2

---

225   CONTINUED: (2)

                 GITTES
      There's no time for you to be
      shocked by the truth, Mrs. Mulwray.
      The coroner's report proves he was
      killed in salt water, just take my
      word for it. Now I want to know
      how it happened and why. I want
      to know before Escobar gets here
      because I want to hang onto my
      license.

                 EVELYN
      -- I don't know what you're talking
      about. This is the most insane...
      the craziest thing I ever...

Gittes has been in a state of near frenzy himself. He gets up, shakes her.

                 GITTES
      Stop it! -- I'll make it easy. --
      You were jealous, you fought, he
      fell, hit his head -- it was an
      accident -- but his girl is a
      witness. You've had to pay her
      off. You don't have the stomach
      to harm her, but you've got the
      money to shut her up. Yes or no?

                 EVELYN
      ... no...

                 GITTES
      Who is she? and don't give me that
      crap about it being your sister.
      You don't have a sister.

Evelyn is trembling.

                 EVELYN
      I'll tell you the truth...

Gittes smiles.

                 GITTES
      That's good. Now what's her name?

                 EVELYN
      -- Katherine.

                    (CONTINUED)

3

---

225   CONTINUED: (3)

                 GITTES
      Katherine?... Katherine who?

                 EVELYN
      -- she's my daughter.

226   Gittes stares at her. He's been charged with anger and when Evelyn says this it explodes. He hits her full in the face. Evelyn stares back at him. The blow has forced tears from her eyes, but she makes no move, not even to defend herself.

                 GITTES
      I said the truth!

                 EVELYN
      -- she's my sister --

Gittes slaps her again.

                 EVELYN
          (continuing)
      -- she's my daughter.

Gittes slaps her again.

                 EVELYN
          (continuing)
      -- my sister.

He hits her again.

                 EVELYN
          (continuing)
      My daughter, my sister --

He belts her finally, knocking her into a cheap Chinese vase which shatters and she collapses on the sofa, sobbing.

                 GITTES
      I said I want the truth.

                 EVELYN
         (almost screaming it)
      She's my sister <u>and</u> my daughter!

                    (CONTINUED)

4

5

6

7

8

9

10

(1–10) **Chinatown**: "It is often through the dialogue that you advance the story and give the audience essential information. In this scene Gittes [Jack Nicholson] confronts Evelyn Mulwray [Faye Dunaway] with the fact that he believes she has murdered her husband. To make it easy Gittes develops this scenario that she was jealous and fought him. It's a highly dramatic scene. Gittes has totally misjudged the situation; the person he assumed was the villain is the heroine. The plot information is delivered by beating it out of her, and the audience does not think 'Holy shit, I'm being given information'. It is thinking how is Gittes going to control himself?"

he might fail. In one passage, a teacher encourages students to yell out "digression, digression", whenever the student who is reading wavers off the point. Caulfield admits that his favourite part of anybody talking is their digressions. People say interesting things while digressing; it's when you really get to know what is on their mind. It is all about reading between the lines when people talk.

In Salinger there is a wonderful use of refrain. Communicating indirectly through refrain is actually the way people talk. "If you know what I mean?" is an abiding refrain in "The Catcher in the Rye". The repetition of refrain in dialogue, beautifully used, can affect you almost like music affects you. In **Angels with Dirty Faces**, Pat O'Brien and James Cagney play two Irish kids; one becomes a priest and the other a criminal. As a little kid you hear Cagney say, "Hey, what do you hear, what do you say?", and it's a sign of his cockiness. He repeats this line throughout the movie. At the end Cagney is on death row, and the priest O'Brien comes to take him on his last walk and Cagney says, "Hey, what do you hear, what do you say?" At that moment, you recall each time that the phrase was said up until then; it has a resonance. It reminds you of where you were with that character and how far you have gone with him. Refrain can be very powerful in dialogue and it works best when it is some colloquial expression that everybody uses without thinking.

To write effective dialogue, it's also essential to listen to how people misuse language. The line from **Shampoo** – "I'm cutting too much hair and losing all my concepts" – was something that a hairdresser actually said to me. I could not have made that line up. It was just uniquely the way this guy talked. It works in the script because it perfectly fits the culture of that time, in a city that was centred on appearance, full of people obsessed with the way they look. Throughout **Shampoo** I use the mantra, "Great. Great". Because if it's not great, God forbid, it's terrible! "How do you like it?" "It's good. It's good". "You hate it". "No, no, it's great, it's great". "Are you sure?" "Oh great, great, yes". The insecurity that causes this attention to appearance in the first place gives rise to and is expressed through the rhetoric. The way in which dialogue expresses and reveals your characters becomes very basic to the story that you are telling.

In contrast, the dialogue in **The Last Detail** was full of swearing, and it almost stopped us getting the film made. The main characters are two older soldiers who escort an army kid to the military prison for eight years' hard time for stealing $40. As they hear the kid's story and how he failed to defend himself from arrest, it becomes evident to these guys that the theft was just a minor emotional disturbance. If the kid had had the least ability to speak up for himself he would not be going to jail. Any swearing in the dialogue was truthful and necessary to the story. The military is famous for its liberal use of scatological language, hence the phrase, "swears like a trooper". When you're in the military you do what you're told and all you can do is swear about it. David Beigelman, the head of Columbia, at one point asked me "...if 20 mother-fuckers wouldn't be more dramatic than 40 motherfuckers". I said that they would be, but the whole point of **The Last Detail** is that the swearing is not dramatic. These men swear – not as an adjunct or underlining to action, but as a substitute for it. It is an indication of their impotency. It is not like when Rhett Butler says, "Frankly, my dear, I don't give a damn", and walks out on Scarlett. In that case, the word and the action are consummate and the swearing is dramatic.

1

2

"I've always considered the original detective movie to be **Oedipus Rex**, and every detective story written ever since to be a kind of substitute for it. Oedipus at the end realises he himself was the villain all along and guilty of killing his father and marrying his mother. The most satisfying detective movies are those in which the villain is right in front of your eyes from the very beginning. (1) In **The Maltese Falcon**, Miss Wonderly comes in for help from Sam Spade and explains that all these terrible people are out to get her. The detective listens, goes through many permutations, comes back and realises that the criminal (Miss Wonderly) has been in front of his eyes from the very beginning." (2–3) "There's no culture in the world that has been more eloquent about saying things indirectly than the Irish, most probably as a result of oppression. The lyrics of 'Nell Flaherty's Drake' (3) tell the tale of a duck that is killed. The song is really about the Irish rebel Robert Emmett (2), who was killed by the British. They couldn't say this directly. Once again, it is all subtext!"

Oh my name it is Nell, and the truth for to tell,
I come from Cootehill which I'll never deny;
I had a fine drake, and I'd die for his sake,
That my grandmother left me, and she going to die.
The dear little fellow, his legs they were yellow;
He could fly like a swallow or swim like a hake
'Til some dirty savage, to grease his white cabbage,
Most wantonly murdered my beautiful drake.

Now, his neck it was green oh, most fit to be seen,
He was fit for a queen of the highest degree.
His body was white, and it would you delight;
He was plump, fat, and heavy, and brisk as a bee.
He was wholesome and sound, he would weight twenty pound,
And the universe 'round I would roam for his sake.
Bad luck to the robber, be he drunk or sober,
That murdered Nell Flaherty's beautiful drake.

May his spade never dig, may his sow never pig,
May each hair in his wig be well thrashed with a flail;
May his turkey not hatch, may the rats eat his meal.
May every old fairy from Cork to Dunleary
Dip him smug and airy in river or lake,
That the eel and the trout, they may dine on the snout
Of the monster that murdered Nell Flaherty's drake.

May his pig never grunt, may his cat never hunt,
May a ghost ever haunt him at dead of the night;
May his hens never lay, may his horse never neigh,
May his goat fly away like an old paper kite.
That the flies and the fleas may the wretch ever tease,
May the piercing March breeze make him shiver an shake;
May a lump of a stick raise the bumps fast and thick
Of the monster that murdered Nell Flaherty's drake.

Now the only good news that I have to infuse
Is that old Paddy Hughs and young Anthony Blake,
Also Johnny Dwyer and Corney Maguire,
They each have a grandson of my darling drake.
My treasure had dozens of nephews and cousins,
And one I must et or my heart it will break;
To set my mind aisy or else I'll run crazy -
So ends the whole song of Nell Flaherty's drake.

3

1

2

3

(1–7) **The Godfather**: Coppola felt that the scene he had written where the mantle of power was passed from Don Vito [Marlon Brando] to his son, Michael [Al Pacino] was not quite right (4–5). He approached Towne and asked him to rewrite this scene (6–7). "People do not like to relinquish power, but there is an interesting variation here in that the Don's reluctance to relinquish it is because this power is so dark and evil that he does not want his son to inherit it. The line, 'I refuse to be a puppet dancing on a string for these guys, I don't apologise for my life', was inspired by the cover for the book 'The Godfather'. When I arrived on set Marlon Brando asked me to read the scene to him. Once he was satisfied that the scene was going to work he really took it apart by having me read it again and stopping me and asking me what each moment meant. It was intimidating, but also a tremendous relief that somebody was paying attention. It encouraged me to keep trying to write that way."

MICHAEL
(coldly)
You're out, Tom.

TOM pauses, thinks...and then he nods in acquiescence. TOM
leaves. MICHAEL looks at NERI.

MICHAEL (CONT'D)
I'm going to talk to my father.
NERI nods, and then leaves.

The DON opens the doors, breathes in the air, and steps
outside.

EXT DAY: THE GARDEN (1955)

DON CORLEONE
I see you have your Luca Brasi.

MICHAEL
I'll need him.

DON CORLEONE
There are men in this world who
demand to be killed. They argue in
gambling games; they jump out of
their cars in a rage if someone so
much as scratches their fender.
These people wander through the
streets calling out "Kill me, kill
me." Luca Brasi was like that. And
since he wasn't scared of death,
and in fact, looked for it...I made
him my weapon. Because I was the
only person in the world that he
truly hoped would not kill him. I
think you have done the same with
this man.

They walk through the DON's vegetable garden. Tomatoes,
peppers, carefully tended, and covered with a silky netting.
MICHAEL follows; the DON turns and looks at him. Then stoops
over to right a tomato plant that had been pushed over.

DON CORLEONE (CONT'D)
Barzini will move against you
first.

MICHAEL
How?

DON CORLEONE
He will get in touch with you
through someone you absolutely
trust. That person will arrange a
meeting, guarantee your safety...

He rises, and looks at Michael...

DON CORLEONE (CONT'D)
...and at that meeting you will be
assassinated.

The DON walks on further.

DON CORLEONE (CONT'D)
Your wife and children...you're
happy with them?

MICHAEL
Yes.

DON CORLEONE
Good.

MICHAEL wants to express something...hesitates, then:

MICHAEL
I've always respected you...

A long silence. The DON smiles at MICHAEL.

DON CORLEONE
And I...you.

EXT DAY: CHURCH (1955)

KAY and MAMA walking from the black car that has just left
them off.

KAY
How is your husband feeling?

MAMA
He's not the same since they shot
him. He lets Michael do all the
work. He just plays the fool with
his garden, his peppers, his
tomatoes, as if he was some peasant
still. But men are like that...

She stops toward the Church.

MAMA (CONT'D)
You come in, too.

KAY shakes her head.

THE DON'S GARDEN

The DON, older looking now, sits with Michael.

VITO CORLEONE
So - Barzini will move against you
first. He'll set up a meeting with
someone that you absolutely trust -
guaranteeing your safety. And at
that meeting, you'll be
assassinated.
I like to drink wine more than I
used to - anyway, I'm drinking
more...

MICHAEL
It's good for you, Pop.

VITO CORLEONE
I don't know - your wife and
children - are you happy with them?

MICHAEL
Very happy...

VITO CORLEONE
That's good. I hope you don't mind
the way I - I keep going over this
Barzini business...

MICHAEL
No, not at all...

VITO CORLEONE
It's an old habit. I spent my life
trying not to be careless - women
and children can be careless, but
not men.
(beat)
How's your boy?

MICHAEL
He's good -

VITO CORLEONE
You know he looks more like you
every day.

MICHAEL
(smiling)
He's smarter than I am. Three years
old, he can read the funny papers

VITO CORLEONE
(laughs)
Read the funny papers -

VITO CORLEONE (CONT'D)
Oh - well - eh, I want you to
arrange to have a telephone man
check all the calls that go in and
out of here - because...

MICHAEL
I did it already, Pop.

VITO CORLEONE
- ya know, cuz it could be
anyone...

MICHAEL
Pop, I took care of that.

VITO CORLEONE
Oh, that's right - I forgot.

MICHAEL
(reaching over, touching
his father)
What's the matter? What's bothering
you? I'll handle it. I told you I
can handle it, I'll handle it.

VITO CORLEONE
(as he stands)
I knew that Santino was going to
have to go through all this. And
Fredo - well -
(after he sits besides
Michael)
- Fredo was - well - But I never -
I never wanted this for you. I work
my whole life, I don't apologize,
to take care of my family. And I
refused - to be a fool - dancing on
the string, held by all those -
bigshots. I don't apologize -
that's my life - but I thought that
- that when it was your time - that
- that you would be the one to hold
the strings. Senator - Corleone.
Governor - Corleone, or
something...

MICHAEL
Another pezzonovante...

VITO CORLEONE
Well - this wasn't enough time,
Michael. Wasn't enough time...

4

5

6

7

screenwriting

(1–4) **The Last Detail**: Two soldiers, Buddusky and Mulhall, escort a boy called Meadows to jail. (3–4) In this scene they have stopped off at a diner where Meadows has ordered a hamburger. "What Buddusky is really saying is stand up for yourself. If you stood up for yourself you wouldn't be going to jail for eight years for stealing $40. In all effective dialogue there is a critical element of subtext."

3

33

EXT. STREET

30   The three emerge from the alcove, walking, two impeccable   30
      sailors and a sloppy one, but they no longer appear as
      prisoner and guards.

      Billy and Mule hitch up their pants, turn up their peacoat
      collars, and drop their hats over their foreheads by
      way of reacting to the cold. Meadows gives a shabby
      imitation of their movements. Buddusky laughs when he
      sees this. He adjusts Meadows' collar. Mule picks up,
      leans over and gives the right tilt to Meadows' hat.
      They saunter off.

INT. HAMBURGER JOINT

31   They sit at the counter. The hamburgers are brought   31
      along with shakes and fries. Buddusky looks at Meadows'
      cheeseburger suspiciously.

                    BUDDUSKY
            Cheese melted enough?

                    MEADOWS
            Sure.

      Buddusky looks at it closely.

                    BUDDUSKY
            Ain't melted at all. Send it
            back.

                    MEADOWS
            No, it's okay, really.

                    BUDDUSKY
            Send the goddam thing back.
            You're paying for it, aren't
            you?

                    MEADOWS
            It's all right, really.

                    BUDDUSKY
            Have it the way you want it.
            Waiter?

                    MEADOWS
            No please -

                    WAITER
            Yes, sir?

                                                              34
31   CONTINUED: 31

                    BUDDUSKY
            Melt the cheese on this for the
            Chief here, will you?

                    WAITER
            Certainly.

      The waiter takes it away.

                    BUDDUSKY
            See, kid, it's just as easy to
            have it the way you want it.

32   CLOSE ON MEADOWS   32
      biting into his cheeseburger.

                    BUDDUSKY
            See what I mean?

      Meadows nods. Buddusky looks over to Mule, pleased with
      himself.

EXT. STREET THE THREE

33   lifting their collars again and putting on their gloves.33

                    MULE
                (moving)
            Better catch that train.

                    BUDDUSKY
            We still got time for a beer.

                    MULE
            Now wait a minute, man -

                    MEADOWS
            I ain't old enough.

                    BUDDUSKY
                (whirling on him)
            You ain't old enough for what?

                    MEADOWS
                (intimidated)
            For a beer.

The opportunity arose to do a film like **The Last Detail** because of changes in the Motion Picture Production Code, known as the Hayes Office. They lifted restrictions on language, as well as on scenes of intimacy and violence. This change was really for economic reasons, because TV had made such inroads into the movie-going audience that they were willing to try anything to recapture some of those people. They wanted to show them something that could not be seen on TV, which really meant something a little more sensational. Whether by accident or design, they ended up finding a whole counterculture. Whereas TV was about wholesomeness and the importance of the family, film came to be about alienation and featured troubled outsiders in search of some sort of meaning after the Vietnam War and the Watergate scandal. Audiences sought answers for who they were or what their problems were in movie theatres.

The Last Detail offered me the chance to bring a level of reality into film that had not been there before. The script dealt with what seemed a not terribly dramatic situation, rather than one of pith and moment. Worlds were not at stake. It was just about how some army kid who stole $40 was escorted to the military prison; in that sense, it was more like **Bicycle Thieves**. The idea was to write about those things that nobody would normally show in a movie. Traditional films about crime would either show somebody committing the crime, the court martial proceeding it or the brutality of being in prison. Those are the dramatic situations. This little picturesque interlude of taking the boy to the prison (which is the whole script of the film) would once have been called "shoe leather" – those scenes that don't seem to have any particular dramatic purpose.

When I was a kid, one of the things that would consistently drive me batty in movies was that whenever somebody pulled up to a hotel, like the Waldorf Astoria in the middle of New York, there was always somewhere in front of the hotel to park. To get on with the serious business of the movie a space was provided for the protagonist. Invariably, whenever movie characters paid the bill in a restaurant, it was always, "Keep the change". As a child, you know Dad doesn't always say, "Hey, keep the change honey", when he's got a family to feed and money is not that easy to come by. These are just cinematic conventions to get around shoe leather. I decided to introduce it into a movie and make an issue out of it. The entire story from start to finish is really shoe leather.

When I was writing **Chinatown**, I incorporated shoe leather into the script from the very beginning. There is a scene where the detective Gittes goes to see a Mr Mulwray at his house, but you do not automatically get to the part where they meet up. Gittes arrives at the big Spanish-style Mulwray home, he walks to the front door and knocks at it, and he hears some squeaking. It feels like a mystery. Then the Chinese butler opens the door. Gittes asks for Mulwray and the butler closes the door in his face. Gittes stands there and he hears some more squeaking and he looks around. Poking out from behind the rear of the Packard is someone using a chamois on the car. The butler returns, opens the door and only then brings him in to see Mulwray. This is all shoe leather but it also establishes a different world, one so quiet that you can hear the squeak of a chamois on the car.

Both these films may be slow at points, but they are still dramatic. The writer can do that. In **2001: A Space Odyssey**, the screen fills with a huge spaceship going slowly

```
                    LUTHER
               (to Billy)
          Bearing two one zero.  About 3
          klicks.
               (into microphone)
          Ethan, we're moments away..

EXT - CLIFFTOP - CLEARING - FIGHT

Ethan and Ambrose rise from the fall.  Ethan jumps up and
sweeps Ambrose, dropping him to the ground.  Ethan begins
strangling Ambrose but gets knocked off, and when they both
stand, Ambrose gets Ethan in a choke hold.

Ambrose hits him and grabs a rock and hits Ethan in the

midsection and the face.  Ethan kicks it out of his hand and
connects with several punches, knocking Ambrose to the
ground. Kneeling, Ambrose pulls a knife from a boot holster
and cuts Ethan across the back and face.  Ambrose dives on
Ethan and theknife is poised above Ethan's eye before Ethan
grabs the knife and clears, holding it out toward Ambrose.

                    AMBROSE
          Go ahead.  Use it Hunt.  It's not a
          bad way to go.  A lot better than
          the way that bitch is going to die.

Ambrose swings again and misses, and Ethan delivers a series
of kicks, leaving Ambrose stunned and barely standing.  Ethan
steps back, and with a running start, strikes Ambrose with a
leaping kick that drops him to the ground and knock the knife
out of his hand.

EXT/INT   IMF HELICOPTER - CLIFFTOP

As they approach in the distance, Billy, Luther and Nyah
finally gain sight of Ethan in hand-to-hand combat.

EXT - CLIFFTOP - CLEARING - FIGHT

Ethan turns and walks away from Ambrose toward the cliff
edge. The copter lands and Luther runs toward Ethan but pulls
up, looking over Ethan's shoulder.  Ambrose has a gun aimed
at Ethan's back.

                    AMBROSE
          Hunt.  You should have killed me.

Neal Hunt's feet is his own gun, obscured from Ambrose's view
by dust from the copter.  Ethan tosses the canister to Luther
and then kicks his gun up out of the dirt and into the air.
He catches it, drops down and fires, killing Ambrose.
```

9

"You can only write within the parameters of the world that you have been lumbered with. In between the rides and the action sequences of **Mission: Impossible II** there is not a lot of time to deal with the nuances of character. Ideally you should be doing that through the action sequences, even though there is limited ability to do so. I think the final script of **Mission** is 84 pages. Action sequences are quicker on the page than dialogue." (1–9) Script excerpt and frames from an action sequence in the film. (10) Towne.

across the screen. That is obviously very dramatic. But you could film a bug going across a tabletop and it would look every bit as big on screen as that spaceship. If there were a compelling reason making the audience desperately curious to know if that bug is going to make it across the table, if you were able to set up that situation, it would be just as dramatic as the spaceship. In **The Last Detail**, all the seemingly picturesque episodes that make up the journey are informed by the unspoken question, "Will the two soldiers let the kid go?" That is a very dramatic question, even if it isn't blatantly obvious. You raise a question that the audience increasingly wants the answer to without ever asking it specifically.

As more than one person has surely said, writing is just re-writing, and that is no more true than it is with screenplays. It is hard work. I think my own writing habits come from working as a fisherman earlier in my life. I write every day until I drop and keep writing until it is finished. A fisherman is out every day until sunset. Everytime he throws his pole in the water it is an act of faith, hoping there is something down there beneath that grey expanse of water. There were fish yesterday, and so he figures he will catch some today. You are not doing anything terribly different as a writer. You think, there's something underneath that grey matter, and you have got to fish it out.

biography

Suso Cecchi D'Amico, daughter of writer and translator Emilio Cecchi, was born in Italy in 1914. Her father worked for a period as artistic director for the Cines studio during the '30s. When his film-maker friends visited their house they would often ask the young D'Amico to look at their screenplays, to see if they would interest young people. At this time D'Amico worked with her father on theatre

suso d'amico

interview

translations, but had written nothing for cinema. One of her father's friends asked her to work on a screenplay of a film with Alberto Moravia and Ennio Flaiano. D'Amico accepted and has continued to write for the cinema ever since. In 1946 she began working with Cesare Zavattini and Vittorio De Sica on a screenplay called 'Bicycle Thieves', telling the story of an impoverished man trying to maintain his dignity in the face of an uncaring society. **Bicycle Thieves (Ladri di Biciclette**, 1948) is perceived as a major work of the Italian neo-realist movement, which presented human problems in natural settings. These films strived for an authenticity that was not only a cinematic style but also a whole social, moral and political philosophy. D'Amico has written over 80 screenplays since 1946. Credits include **Miracle in Milan (Miracolo a Milano**, Vittorio De Sica, 1951), **Senso** (1954), **Rocco and His Brothers (Rocco e i suoi Fratelli**, 1960), **The Leopard (Il Gattopardo**, 1963, Luchino Visconti), **Salvatore Giuliano** (Francesco Rosi, 1961) and **Jesus of Nazareth** (Franco Zeffirelli, 1977). Recent work includes **The Sky Will Fall** (Andrea and Antonio Frazzi, 2000).

It was circumstances that brought my generation to cinema as the means to tell our story. I had lived through 20 years of fascism and the Second World War. Throughout this period there had been very heavy censorship of the arts by the state, and therefore the films made were not at all realistic. If there had been the amount of newspapers that there are today, perhaps we would have become journalists. As it was we wrote films. We wrote about the society we lived in and its problems. Times were difficult. There was no theatre and no money to pay actors so we chose people from the streets and we were open to improvisation. This became a style and critics called it neo-realism. These films appeared much more authentic than what had gone before.

I've always lived among intellectuals. My father was a writer, my mother was a painter and our house was full of the intelligentsia of the period. We all read a lot when I was a child – there was no TV or even radio. It was a completely different life for young people then. My father had a very big library and was a great guide in reading. He would choose a

(1) D'Amico with director Luchino Visconti. (2–5) **Senso**: "The opera was a big tradition of storytelling in Italy. Visconti directed 21 operas, half of them by Verdi. He was attracted by their spectacle, melodrama and sensuality – qualities he brought to his film-making to create a cinematic equivalent of opera music. **Senso** is melodramatic and full of aria like an opera. That is why it begins with one, to give the idea of what we intended to do with it."

book for me to read and when it was finished we would talk about it. Then he gave me another. I remember discussions between my father and his friends who thought that I had been given some books too young – I was reading Dostoevsky when I was 13 years old! We were also mad about the movies. I would go to the cinema in the afternoon and stay until dinner time; watching the same feature again and again.

One of the first scripts I wrote was "Bicycle Thieves" for Vittorio De Sica. The story for **Bicycle Thieves** came from a little book written by an Italian painter called Luigi Bartolini. We bought the rights for this book. It was a chronicle which documented life at that time, showing the desperation of some people and their impoverished living conditions. The story is about a man who spends a day in Rome meeting up with certain people and it ends with the man heading off home after he has lost his bicycle. Not a single scene from the book ends up in the completed film. [Cesare] Zavattini had thought it was enough to recreate this chronicle of a day going by, but I felt the story needed a dramatic construction. We decided to insert events that would function inside the general architecture of the story. I proposed that the man would steal a bicycle and that his child would see this terrible event.

To research the script we spoke with people who lived in those desperate conditions and we used lines of dialogue that we actually heard. Real people were the actors and we had real locations. We tried to recreate reality in an attempt to attain authenticity. It was essential that the script would be authentic. Many ideas came from speaking and staying with the people who lived this life in Rome. My interest in what I saw always overcame any unpleasantness or shock. I once wrote a film that took place inside a women's prison, and met a woman who was inside doing time for robbery. To this day we maintain a friendship. While researching scripts, you have to get to know people that you would not normally meet.

For example, before writing the fortune-teller scene in **Bicycle Thieves**, I went with De Sica, Zavattini and De Sica's assistant to visit an actual fortune-teller, to research how they behave. This was our approach to research. This fortune-teller received people from two o'clock until six o'clock in the evening – at six she stopped, and if you had not talked with her then you came back the next day. We were there for three days waiting! Finally, when it was our turn to speak, De Sica's assistant, Gerardo Guerrieri, went to "Battusa" and said to her, "They've stolen my bicycle". The fortune-teller looked at him with suspicion, because everybody else there had experienced real tragedy – they had lost a whole family or they had cancer. De Sica thought that it was bad luck to have done this, and he went to the lady the next day and asked her if she would like to act the part of the fortune-teller in the film. She refused. De Sica was an extraordinarily superstitious person, so he then decided not to include the scene at all. We protested to him so much that eventually it remained in the film.

The most important thing about these films was the theme and content, not constructing the plot structure. We wanted to write documents that would show people how things were. **Rocco and His Brothers** was about the emigration of poor land workers from the south to the north of Italy. The harsh post-war environment made their integration even more difficult. The people didn't understand each other, because there were two languages within Italy: southern and northern Italian. In such conditions people can end up doing anything.

1

2

3

4

5

265.

STRADINA VIA FLAMINIA

–

Antonio ormai vicino alla bicicletta la oltrepassa; guarda dentro il
portone.

–

Vede in fondo all'andito due uomini che parlano.

–

Oltrepassa il portone, sosta un
momento. Poi torna indietro e
guarda di nuovo i due uomini che
parlano in fondo all'andito. Va
verso la bicicletta. Gli si mette
vicino e d'un tratto la inforca.

–

Per l'emozione gli sfugge un pe-
dale, sta per cadere, mette un
piede a terra, fa uno sforzo e si
rimette in equilibrio, parte, for-
za i pedali.

–

Dal portone escono immediatamente

6

266.

due persone, un operaio e un por-
tiere.
Si guardano tra di loro, hanno un
attimo di esitazione, si mettono
a correre, gridano:

GRIDA
Al ladro! Al ladro!

–

Dal fondo della strada, dalla parte dove Antonio si è diretto, gli
viene incontro un gruppetto di
gente. Antonio è costretto a vol-
tare. Prende una via traversa.

–

Gli inseguitori aumentano. Ai due
se ne aggiungono altri. Gruppi di
gente che passa si voltano curiosi.

CLAMORI
Ferma! Ferma! Al ladro!

–

Antonio ha preso una strada pa-
rallela a quella dove ha rubato
la bicicletta e ora sbocca di cor-
sa sulla Flaminia.

–

I due che l'inseguono hanno intui-
to la manovra di Antonio; si danno

7

D'Amico felt that the original documentary chronicle on which **Bicycle Thieves** was based needed some dramatic structure. She suggested that the son would see his father steal a bike (1–9) "We made **Bicycle Thieves** with non-professional actors, as they gave the film an authenticity we could not have got by using professional ones. We wanted to make something as different and as real as possible. **Rome, Open City** had already been a big success in the States, and American actors started to come to see Rome out of curiosity. Cary Grant offered to play the lead role in **Bicycle Thieves**. We thought it would be ridiculous to see Cary Grant going out to steal the bicycle, but it was very difficult to say no because we knew he would open up sources of money."

I wanted to show how desperation can bring anyone to commit a crime. This is the moral of the film. We decided to make **Rocco** more like a novel as opposed to the documentary chronicle that was **Bicycle Thieves**. We had professional actors and did not use improvisation. These were definite changes, but authenticity was still my main aim. We went to Milan and spent time there with people who had emigrated from the south. We based the script on our experiences there. We discovered that youths boxed just to gain a few lira and that boxing was a source of entertainment for the poor. This is how boxing became an important backdrop in the movie.

There are five screenwriters, including the director Visconti, credited on **Rocco and His Brothers**. [Massimo] Franciosa and [Pasquale Festa] Campanile were two southerners who we used on **Rocco** to write the local dialect for the southern characters. However, in the end, we found that it did not work having the characters speak in dialect and we had them speak Italian with a slight accent. Often in American films when there is only one person credited, many people may have had a hand in the script. We are more generous and give everyone a credit. On films with two or three writers there may be one who is good at the construction, or one who is good at dialogue, or one who writes the treatment quicker. In comedy it's very useful to work in twos or threes. If you don't all laugh at the joke, you know it doesn't work.

The Leopard, written for Visconti in 1963, was based on the book of the same name by Giuseppe Tomasi di Lampedusa. It is about the end of an epoch in society when the dying aristocracy must learn to change everything in order not to dissolve. To write about this I frequented the company of the Sicilian aristocracy, whom I had come to know very well when

I was on location for the film **Salvatore Giuliano**. In attempting to be faithful to the meaning of the book, the film script turned out very differently. In the book, the last two chapters are flash-forwards to 30 and 60 years ahead of the rest of the narrative, describing the death of a prince and then the decline of his aristocratic society. When adapting the novel we decided, at Visconti's suggestion, to cut out these final chapters. We felt the only way I could adapt the book was to set it in one time period. If you had a story that stops then flashes forward 30 years and then another 30, it would not have worked. The aim of an honest screen adaptation is to impart the meaning, style and character of a book.

Whereas De Sica created a naturalistic reproduction of reality, Visconti was always melodramatic and operatic. The two directors' interpretations of reality are completely different because they have two distinct personalities. As the writer I find it important to adapt to the personality of the film's director. I work like an artisan and an artisan must know the needs of the person asking for his work. This attitude has allowed me to write many different kinds of film. I worked with Visconti on ten films and I reached a stage where we hardly needed to talk because I knew already what he wanted. Since I always work closely with directors I know, my characters normally turn out similar in the final film to how I've conceived them in the script. I often discuss with directors how a part will be cast. I've been very lucky. One of the best screenplays I wrote was with [Ettore] Giannini called "The City Stands Trial". However, the casting of the main protagonist was a disaster. We thought that it should be an unknown, because the script was about a little man who discovers the huge corruption in a town. However, the producers imported Amedeo Nazzari who was the premier

1

4

2

3

(1–3) **Rocco and His Brothers**: "Sometimes when you know who is going to play a part, you keep the idea of this present as you write the script. I like the Nadia character in **Rocco**; her pride, her unhappiness and character. When I wrote the script I knew Annie Girardot (who played Nadia) as a theatre actress, and her characteristics helped create this portrait of a woman (3). When I wrote **Rocco** we knew that we would have Alain Delon (Rocco), Renato Salvatori (Simone) and Girardot (Nadia)." (4) "Dostoevsky is a fantastic author for inspiring character. Prince Myshkin in Dostoevsky's 'The Idiot' is an innocent in a corrupt world whose good acts provoke evil. He is the basis for Rocco. Nastasia Npovna from 'The Idiot' is the Nadia of **Rocco**. I always thought the Russians are very similar to the southern Italians – full of sentiment. '*Il sentimento è piú forte della raggione*' ('Emotions are stronger than reason'), they say."

1

3

4

2

5

6

(1–6) "The final two chapters of **The Leopard** were dropped in the film adaptation. They described the death of the Prince (played by Burt Lancaster) and the decay of his aristocratic family. Instead, the sense of death and decay had to be conveyed in the final ball sequence."

1

2

actor at that time: beautiful, tall and well-groomed. Both the screenplay and the direction are very good, but I was always disappointed with this choice of casting.

We in the old generation were never told to write something so that it would be a certain success. The idea of aiming for success is something that came much later. Such films are less authentic because writers think that they must write something different in order to have a success in Japan, in America, in France. That has no sense. We did what we thought we should do. I remember when I received a note written by an American friend about the success of **Bicycle Thieves** in the States. I was surprised because the success was something I had not expected. When the Italian films started to be successful abroad, the American studios offered me a long contract to work in the States. Maybe after staying

there many years I could have written an American story. I don't know. I never accepted their offer. I write about that which I know to be true, and address it to people that I really know. I write about Italy and its problems, and I write it for my Italian neighbour.

There are really no rules when writing a good story. When I begin, the intention is always to tackle problems of society, then little by little it becomes a private story. I always write about my experience; even in the most fantastic tale there is some autobiographical truth. I have always tried very hard to write authentically about the problems of society, but since the '70s, when the *Brigate Rosse* period began, I don't really know what is going on in society anymore. The world's a pretty strange place these days. We can always tell the story of reality, but the political situation in Italy is now so

3

4

ambiguous that it is perplexing. I would be worried about representing it in a way that a lot of people wouldn't like.

I think that cinema and movies have been bad for morality. All day long on TV children see violence and watch heroes who kill. I think that a screenwriter should be aware of how much they are responsible for people's behaviour. I am really a strict censor of myself and of what I write. I am terrified by what you can do with images. I do not accept stories that I think could be dangerous. Screenwriting is a very important craft and I am completely aware of my responsibility. My writing has enriched my life. It is my aim that it will enrich other people's lives.

(1–4) "I was very pleased with **Jesus of Nazareth**, because it was such a simple and straightforward piece, and faithful to the original text. I think the words of Jesus and the Evangelists are really beautiful. The Gospels tell what is probably the most influential and important story for Western civilisation. They are more real than the histories of Caesar, although we don't have any tangible proof of their authenticity."

biography

Atom Egoyan was born in 1960 in Cairo. His parents named him at a time when Egypt's first nuclear power plant was built. They were Armenian refugees who decided to leave political unrest behind them and moved from Cairo to Victoria, Canada in 1963. Victoria, often referred to as the last bastion of the British Empire, created an illusion of being an English town – complete with Beefeaters. The absurdity of

atom egoyan

interview

Egoyan's environment extended to his life at home: his father ran a furniture store and taught evening courses in interior design, which would culminate in a visit to the Egoyan household. "Twice a year I was exposed to this parade of strangers walking through our house, looking into the bedrooms, and looking at how the house was designed. My parents were very specific about how they wanted me to be behind my desk and pretend as if everything was quite normal." This unusual upbringing would help inform the world-view of Egoyan's stories. At the age of 13 he started writing plays. Later, as a college student in Toronto, Egoyan devoted himself to reconnecting with the culture of his family; all the while continuing to write drama. When one of his plays was turned down by the Trinity College Dramatic Society, Egoyan made it as a short film, and so began his career as screenwriter and director. His original screenplays include those for **Speaking Parts** (1989), **The Adjuster** (1991), **Exotica** (1994) and **Ararat** (2002), all of which he directed. He has adapted Russell Bank's 'The Sweet Hereafter' (1997) and William Trevor's 'Felicia's Journey' (1999).

While there are many formulaic approaches to writing a screenplay, I try to deploy alternate means of gaining access to the experiences that my characters are going through. I design my stories so that viewers can formulate their own version of events, as opposed to being passive recipients of a set of formulas. I am drawn to situations that are complex and hidden in mystery, and writing screenplays that unravel both the shrouded circumstances that have informed my characters' lives, and that reveal the reasons why these events have been suppressed and denied.

With a traditional structured narrative, the audience waits for certain familiar beats or turns that indicate where the narrative is going. But when a narrative doesn't offer those familiar signs, the audience doesn't know what to expect – they are in a very different place where they are completely disarmed. Some viewers reject the story at this point, but for the viewers who can trust the film they can venture into completely new territory; where they are activated by new and innovative ways for narrative to insinuate itself into their experience. By engaging with the story like this, the film becomes experiential to the viewer – it filters through the viewer's unconscious. The non-linear narrative can allow the viewer to explore, dismiss or engage with a character and their situation in a way that a traditional narrative cannot.

It's not that I'm trying to reject the predominant, traditional way screenplays are structured; the structure I employ is one that comes about organically. Hollywood studios send me a lot of scripts that have the same non-linear structure as I employ, but there is usually some device set up at the beginning to explain the fractured narrative. For example, a film like **Memento**, which I thought was a very exciting film, is more commercial than my work because the reason for the central character's fractured sense of time is explained. As an audience watching such a film you're given licence, in a conventional way, to forfeit your expectations for such a film – the device of the narrative is fully explained. However, this approach to narrative is not as exciting to me as those types of films where that explanation is not given as something concrete, but rather it is the result of the character's psychological state.

My stories often deal with characters that are shattered, and are trying to rebuild themselves. In my approach to structuring a screenplay, I try to create a situation where the viewer is trying to rebuild and formulate what makes up these people's reality, at the same time as my characters' own fractured reality becomes formulated. Conventional screenplays are constructed in such a way as to allow the audience to identify and understand each character and their motivations. This is usually established within the first 20 minutes of these dramas. For me, these moments where you

are trying to establish each character's relationship to each other are the most exhilarating moments in any drama. A scriptwriter can create a sense of intrigue when the audience is introduced to a character grappling with their own sense of identity. There is an inherent mystery to any meeting of people, and I try and make these moments of contact as thick with subtext and innuendo as possible.

For instance, in **Exotica**, there's a scene where Francis Brown is driving a young woman home. We've seen him spend the evening at a stripper bar with a dancer dressed as a schoolgirl. The next time we see him, he's in a car with this young girl – you assume she is a prostitute. However, at the end of the scene, he says to her, "Say hello to your dad". It's not the line you would expect, and it throws into question your presuppositions of what that scene was about. My screenplays often deal with notions of identity, and I feel that such stories are thrown into sharper focus by characters that are negotiating their right to exist. This plays back into the viewer's negotiation with these characters in terms of whether or not, and by what measure, they are expected to identify with them.

I've found that an audience can identify with a character so emphatically that it becomes possible for them to buy into whatever delusions that character may have. In **The Sweet Hereafter**, for example, I was trying to explore, through the character of Nicole, how someone who is a victim of incest manages to deny the experience she is going through. It struck me that very often when sexual abuse is represented, it is shown from the point of view of the victim after the fact, at a point when they are able to express their anger and rage. However, as violent an idea as it might be, there are situations

3

4

```
                      MISS CALLIGARY
             No, but I bring security with me.
             Security of mind and heart.  Security
             of purpose.

                        OLD WOMAN
             I don't want no Bible.

The OLD WOMAN closes the door.  MISS CALLIGARY turns around,
and notices FELICIA at the bus stop, her head in her hands,
the two green carrier bags beside her.

CUT TO:

INT. 3 DUKE OF WELLINGTON -- DAY

HILDITCH is preparing himself dinner, while speaking on the
phone.  The voice at the other end of the speaker phone is
matter-of-fact and cold.  HILDITCH is watching one of his
MOTHER's cooking shows as he speaks, again repeating every
gesture that she makes.  The sound is turned off the
television.

                         VOICE
             Who's making inquiries about this
             soldier?

                       HILDITCH
             I'm a family friend.  There's been
             an emergency.  The young man's
             father's been in an accident.

                         VOICE
             What are you asking me?

                       HILDITCH
             The family's uncertain which barracks
             the lad's stationed at owing to the
             father being unconscious in a
             hospital.  We're ringing around all
             barracks in the area.

                         VOICE
             Name and rank?

                       HILDITCH
             Lysaght, J.  A squaddy I'd say he
             is.

                         VOICE
             A what?
```

1

```
                       HILDITCH
             A private.

A pause, while the name is searched.  HILDITCH uses the time
to edge up the volume of the television, straining to catch
his MOTHER's instructions.

                         VOICE
             We have a Lysaght here.  We'll pass
             the message on after fatiques.

                       HILDITCH
             Oh no, it would be better if the
             family broke the news to the lad.
             Now that we know where he is we'll
             contact him pronto.

Something on the cooking show catches HILDITCH's attention.
He hangs up the phone as he sees an image of himself - as a
boy (YOUNG HILDITCH) - join his MOTHER on the show.

                         MOTHER
                   (on the television)
             Now, does this young man listen to
             his mother?

YOUNG HILDITCH is painfully shy of the T.V. camera.  He
manages a nod.

ANGLE ON

HILDITCH as he watches the television, mesmerized by this
image.  He also nods.

ANGLE ON

The cooking show.  HILDITCH's MOTHER continues.

                       MOTHER (CONT'D)
             So let's talk about preparation.
             You must always be prepared, Joey.
             Now, this girl's departure has
             dismayed you, hasn't it?

ANGLE ON

HILDITCH nodding.  He is on the verge of tears.  Over his
image his MOTHER's voice is heard.

                       MOTHER (CONT'D)
             And so you must prepare, Joey.
             Prepare for her return.
```

2

(1–2) Script excerpts from **Felicia's Journey** exploring the relationship between Hilditch (Bob Hoskins) and his deceased mother. "I'll never forget reading this half a sentence in William Trevor's original novel, which is just a beautiful glimpse of what happened between mother and son – "'Be nice, dear," in the special voice, the promise that the request will never be made again, broken every time.' The problem with adapting the book is that if you touch on incest, it becomes very heavy handed, it becomes a whole statement, and I don't think either William Trevor or myself would have wanted that explanation to be as prominent as that. So I had to find something else to imply the nature of the relationship between them. I introduced a cookery programme that the mother's character used to present (3). The programme is long since discarded, but Hilditch (4) finds the videos. Hilditch never received his mother's gaze, but through looking at these videos, he feels he can somehow recover it. This activity was very emotionally loaded to me – it wasn't so in the book – but I found it a very profound way of dealing with the nature of his pain, his anguish – something which appeared to be comforting him but which was accelerating his torment."

1

3

2

4

A recurring theme in many of Egoyan's films is voyeurism and the power of media. In **Speaking Parts** (1–2), a woman watches video after video of a young actor with whom she is obsessed, and in **Next of Kin** (3–4), a boy enters another family's life as their long-lost son, after seeing their plight on a video recording made with a therapist. In 2000, Egoyan directed Samuel Beckett's existentialist play 'Krapp's Last Tape' (5–6).

5

6

where a victim of incest convinces themselves that the abuser is somehow loving them, and that the abuse is somehow an extension of that love. This is a profoundly disturbing situation, but I needed to find a language that would communicate Nicole's denial of the traumatic experiences she has with her father. So through much of the introduction into their relationship, the viewer is led to believe that they are "normal" lovers. It is only gradually revealed that they are father and daughter.

At the end of the film, Nicole, the sole young survivor of a bus crash, must testify how the local school bus drove onto the lake. The night before Nicole gives her deposition, Billy – a local truck driver – pleads with Nicole's father not to proceed with the lawsuit, believing it will destroy the community. Nicole's father is reluctant to walk away from the case, believing they will receive substantial compensation. At the deposition, Nicole lies and scuppers any chance of payment from the court. Audiences generally thought that Nicole lied because she believed Billy, not because of her father. They had seen the abuse on screen, but had not absorbed it for what it was, because it is presented from the point of view of someone that is denying the experience. Because of this, the viewer too can deny the experience. It's a very interesting dynamic, and I understand how some people can completely reject my approach because they don't want to feel so close to certain experiences when they're watching a movie.

Traditionally, we tend as viewers to project ourselves onto characters in films, to make their dialogue easy to understand and assimilate. My characters don't possess a mastery of language, they have found that language has betrayed them in some way so they're very cautious about what they choose to

say. In writing dialogue, I try to get at the very essential nature of what it is they are trying to communicate, or not communicate to each other. I strip away every extraneous word; I find when I distil things to that extent, the dialogue becomes extraordinarily concentrated; it becomes very loaded and uncomfortable. This loaded dialogue creates a tension for the viewer – I find it really fascinating when the dialogue is so loaded that the viewer will try and negotiate the dialogue's possible subtextual meaning.

The way in which we find out about a character's "backstory" is as crucial as the details of their lives. A play that has always captured me in regards to its unique method of exposition is Samuel Beckett's "Krapp's Last Tape". The play concerns a 70-year-old man, who every year, on his birthday, makes the decision to tape his reflections on the previous year. And on this particular birthday, he listens to a tape of himself made 30 years ago. Listening to that 40-year-old version of himself, he hears himself reflecting on a tape that he had heard of himself at the age of 25, and in this very simple action, a number of things about his life are revealed. I found the fact that someone would decide to archive their experience in that way to be very interesting. I was fascinated by Krapp performing an activity that is meant to comfort him, but actually torments him, and it is a form of torture that he inflicts on himself. I feel it is through examination of the activity the character is involved in that he reveals himself to us, and further explains why and how he is engaged in the activity. Similarly, many of my own characters involve themselves in a process that they believe gives some sense of meaning to their lives; a process they believe is therapeutic but in fact, only extends their mourning or grief.

3

4

FRANCIS
I mean. it's difficult for me to
tell. I never had much of a musical
education myself. But her teacher
thinks she's really talented.
Actually, we're thinking of getting
her a better piano. A baby grand.
Isn't that a funny name? Baby grand.
Sort of a contradiction in terms.
What do you call it when that
happens? When two words sort of
cancel each other out?

FRANCIS looks over at CHRISTINA. She is staring out the window,
lost in her thoughts.

FRANCIS
What's the matter?

CHRISTINA
What?

FRANCIS
Where's your mind?

CHRISTINA
I was just thinking.

FRANCIS
About what?

CHRISTINA
Just the way you talk about her. You
get so excited. It's nice.

FRANCIS
I'm sure your parents talk that way
about you.

CHRISTINA
I don't think so.

FRANCIS
I do.

CHRISTINA
What makes you so sure?

FRANCIS
You're a very responsible young
woman.

CHRISTINA
Responsible to what?

FRANCIS
To whatever it is you believe you
have to do.

CHRISTINA
Like what?

FRANCIS
Well, Lisa loves when you come over
to babysit for example. She says
that you really listen to her.

CHRISTINA
That's nice. She listens to me too.

Pause. FRANCIS looks over to CHRISTINA.

FRANCIS
She doesn't think you're very happy.

CHRISTINA
I'm not.

FRANCIS
Christina, if there's anything you
ever want to talk about, anything
about what might be happening at
home, you know that I'm here.

CHRISTINA looks at FRANCIS and nods.

CUT TO:

118) EXTERIOR. CHRISTINA'S HOUSE. DUSK.

The car comes to a stop. CHRISTINA watches FRANCIS as he removes
his wallet and hands her some money.

CHRISTINA
Thanks.

Pause.

7

8

2

5

6

CHRISTINA
I really enjoy these drives home, Mr
Brown.

Pause. FRANCIS smiles at CHRISTINA.

FRANCIS
Are you available next Thursday?

CHRISTINA
I think so.

FRANCIS
My wife will give you a call.

CHRISTINA nods, smiles at FRANCIS, and closes the door behind
her. FRANCIS watches until she gets to the house. At the door,
CHRISTINA turns around and waves at FRANCIS. FRANCIS smiles, and
waves back.

CHRISTINA enters her home.

The End. May 18, 1993

(1–9) **Exotica**: Stills of the strip club Exotica where the character Christina works (1–2). "While writing the final scene (3–9), in the final draft of **Exotica**, it occurred to me that Christina was Francis' daughter's babysitter. I think you can feel that this decision, to have Christina be the babysitter, is a result of circumstance as opposed to being in my mind from the outset and writing everything back from that moment. It was a rare situation where the screenplay was able to reflect an urgency and sense of spontaneity and revelation that were the result of the actual writing process, as opposed to something that was artificially generated."

9

1

"The character of Gulliver has fascinated me; someone like Mitchell Stephens [Ian Holm] in **The Sweet Hereafter** (1), completely different from those around him but who has an image of himself as a person able to put to rest some of the latent tensions that inform that society. I'm interested in the character who gives themselves that responsibility. It's not necessarily something they even feel genuinely committed to but it gives them a sense of utility." (2) Still of Egoyan on location for **The Sweet Hereafter** and (3) portrait of playwright Harold Pinter. "One of the first pieces of drama I encountered that used a non-linear approach was Harold Pinter's 'Betrayal'. The play is a tale of adultery with three central characters told backwards – the first scene takes place in spring 1977 and the last in winter 1968, and it chronicles a nine-year extramarital affair. I found the idea of reverse chronology very inspiring, as it demanded that I question my presuppositions about the characters as the play developed. Pinter's plays were very powerful for me because they allow us to engage in the psychological process of recovery that the characters are also sifting through."

2

3

I am intrigued by characters who have jobs or occupations that allow them to deal with their neuroses in a socially acceptable way. It might be the character's decision to seek employment as a film censor or an insurance adjuster (**The Adjuster**), an auditor (**Exotica**) or a customs officer. (The French have a term, *déformation professionnelle*, meaning if you do a job for a long enough time, it begins to affect your character.) Once I've actually determined a circumstance or a job, I try to think of what it is that might attract someone to be in that circumstance; what personal demons do they have that they can somehow negotiate through their job? Professional credentials allow them to express actions that would otherwise be socially unacceptable and they have a patina of anonymity with which they are given licence to other characters' lives.

In the case of Francis Brown in **Exotica**, rather than look at how being in a strip club could change him, I formed his character based on that which would bring someone (Francis) to that club in the first place. Towards the end of the film it is revealed that Francis' daughter was murdered and he was, for a time, suspected of killing her. Shortly after his child's killer is arrested, his wife dies in a car crash – Francis' brother, with whom she was having an affair, drove the car and survived the crash. Francis ritualistically frequents Exotica to see Christina, his daughter's former babysitter, perform. Francis walked into that club one day and he saw Christina performing there, and at that point he had to make a decision – he could either run out, or stay. Francis stayed, but the audience doesn't see that scene, although typically, it would. In **Exotica**, it exists only in the viewer's imagination.

Any person who involves themselves in the process of writing a screenplay does so out of a response to some order in the world that they cannot change. I can create characters that are able to question or determine a universe that would not otherwise exist. As a writer, one is in an extraordinary position to explore creative choices in a way that no-one else in the whole film-making process can. You can allow your imagination to examine any number of routes that a character might take. Like Robert Frost's two roads, your character can take one path or the other. If your character travels down one road, and you decide that you don't agree with the way things unfold, he may walk back and explore the other road. For example, while writing the **Exotica** screenplay, it became clear that Thomas' character (who runs an exotic pet shop), was overtly flirting with Francis' character (who is working as Thomas' accountant), and an explicit sexual relationship developed between the two of them. However, this direction didn't serve the thrust of the drama, and so I rejected it. Even so, as a writer, once you have explored and rejected this path with your character, the tangent remains with you, and informs the final formation of that character.

I know that the stories I write can be challenging to audiences and sometimes the energy fails to connect. But I feel that ultimately, if you have a very high expectation of your audience, and you know exactly what it is you are trying to express through the medium of film, there will always be an audience for you.

picture credits

Courtesy of The Ronald Grant Archive: p2 **Breakfast at Tiffany's**, Paramount Pictures (also on p29); p6 **Schindler's List**, Universal Pictures/Amblin (also on p46); p12 **The Last Temptation of Christ**, Universal Pictures; p16 **The Last Temptation of Christ**, Universal Pictures (1–4); p18 **Taxi Driver**, Columbia Pictures (1–3); p19 **American Gigolo**, Universal Pictures; p19 **Light Sleeper**, Fine Line Features (5); p22 **Affliction**, Largo Entertainment (1–4); p24 **Bus Stop**, 20th Century Fox; p29 **Breakfast at Tiffany's**, Paramount Pictures (2–4); p30 **The Seven Year Itch**, 20th Century Fox (1–3); p32–3 **The Seven Year Itch**, 20th Century Fox (1–4); p35 **The Manchurian Candidate**, United Artists (3, 4); p36 **Bus Stop**, 20th Century Fox (2); p37 **Bus Stop**, 20th Century Fox (4); p38 **Schindler's List**, Universal Pictures/Amblin (1); p41 **Searching for Bobby Fischer**, Paramount Pictures/Channel Four Films (1, 2); p42 **Searching for Bobby Fischer**, Paramount Pictures/Channel Four Films (4); p46 **Schindler's List**, Universal Pictures/Amblin (1); p49 **Schindler's List**, Universal Pictures/Amblin (7); p50 **A Civil Action** © Touchstone Pictures. All rights reserved. (1); p52 **The Boxer**, Universal Pictures/Hell's Kitchen Films, photography by Frank Connor; p56 **Some Mother's Son**, Rank/Castle-Rock-Turner/Hell's Kitchen Films (1, 2); p59 **In the Name of the Father**, Universal Pictures/Hell's Kitchen Films (3–5); p61 **In the Name of the Father**, Universal Pictures/Hell's Kitchen Films (8, 9); p62–3 **My Left Foot**, RTE/Granada/Ferndale Films (1–5); p64 **All the President's Men**, Warner Bros.; p67 **The Princess Bride**, MGM/Buttercup Films (3–6); p70 **Misery**, Castle Rock Entertainment (1–3); p73 **All the President's Men**, Warner Bros. (1–3); p76 **Belle de Jour**, Paris Film; p79 **The Phantom of Liberty**, Fox-Rank/Greenwich (7, 8); p80–1 **Un Chien Andalou**, RGA (1–16); p83 **Belle de Jour**, Paris Film (1–3); p87 **The Tin Drum**, Argos Films (7–13); p88–9 **Danton**, Gaumont International (1–4); p90 **Kuroneko**, Toho; p92 **Children of Hiroshima**, Kindai Eiga Kyokai/Mingei (2–4, 6); p94 **Onibaba**, Toho/Kindai Eiga Kyokai/Tokyo Eiga (9); p95 **Onibaba**, Toho/Kindai Eiga Kyokai/Tokyo Eiga (10, 12); p97 **Stagecoach**, Walter Wanger Productions (2); p97 **Some Like it Hot**, MGM/Mirisch Co. (3); p97 portrait of Molière (5); p97 portrait of Chekhov (6); p126 **The Double Life of Véronique**, Canal +; p130 **Three Colours: Red**, MK2/CED/France 3/CAB Productions/Canal + (1); p130 **Three Colours: White**, MK2/CED/France 3/CAB Productions/Canal + (3); p135 **Three Colours Red**, MK2/CED/France 3/CAB Productions/Canal + (1, 4); p135 **Three Colours: Blue**, MK2/CED/France 3/CAB Productions/Canal + (2); p135 **Three Colours: White**, MK2/CED/France 3/CAB Productions/Canal + (3, 5); p136 **The Double Life of Véronique**, Canal + (2); p136 **A Short Film about Love**, Zespol Filmowy 'Tor'/Film Polski (4); p137 **A Short Film about Killing**, Zespol Filmowy 'Tor'/Film Polski (5); p137 **Dekalog 1**, Polish TV (6); p138 **Mission: Impossible II**, Paramount Pictures; p145 **The Maltese Falcon**, Warner Bros. (1); p146 **The Godfather**, Paramount Pictures (1–3); p148 **The Last Detail**, Columbia Pictures (1, 2); p152 **Rocco and His Brothers**, Titanus; p154 **Senso**, Lux (2–5); p159 **Rocco and His Brothers**, Titanus (1–3); p160–1 **The Leopard**, Titanus (1–6); p162–3 **Jesus of Nazareth**, ITC (1–4); p164 **Exotica**, © Ego Film Arts, photography by Johnnie Eisen; p167 **Felicia's Journey**, © Icon Productions (3); p171 **Exotica**, © Ego Film Arts, photography by Johnnie Eisen (2); p172 portrait of Atom Egoyan on the set of **The Sweet Hereafter**, © Ego Film Arts, photography by Johnnie Eisen (2).

Courtesy of The Bridgeman Art Library: p75 'View of Toledo' by El Greco (Domenico Theotocopuli 1541–1614), Metropolitan Museum of Art, New York, USA/Index/Bridgeman Art Library (4); p84 'The Robing of the Bride' (1940) by Max Ernst (1891–1976), Solomon R. Guggenheim Museum, New York, USA/Bridgeman Art Library, © ADAGP, Paris and DACS, London 2003 (3); p97 'Kamezo as the Warrior Monk, in a scene from "Sembouzakura" at the Ichimura Theatre' (1856) (pen, ink and w/c on paper) by Utagawa Kunisada (1786–1864), Royal Asiatic Society, London, UK/Bridgeman Art Library (4); p159 portrait of Fyodor Dostoevsky (1821–1881) (1872) by Vasili Grigorevich Perov (1832–82), Tretyakov Gallery, Moscow, Russia/Bridgeman Art Library (4).

Visual material contributed by Paul Schrader: p13 portrait shot; p15 (1–3).

Visual material contributed by George Axelrod: p29 (1) photography by Bob Willoughby; p30 (4, 5); p34 **The Manchurian Candidate**, with thanks and acknowledgement to United Artists; p35 (2, 5), with thanks and acknowledgement to United Artists; p36 (1, 3).

Visual material contributed by Steven Zaillian: p41 (3, 4), with thanks and acknowledgement to Fred and Bonnie Waitzkin; p42 (1); p43 (2, 3); p44 (1, 2), with thanks and acknowledgement to Universal Pictures/Amblin; p46 (2–4), with thanks and acknowledgement to Poldek Pfefferberg; p46 (5), with thanks and acknowledgement to Universal Pictures/Amblin; p48 (1–4); p49 (5, 6), with thanks and acknowledgement to Oskar Schindler; p50 (2) photography by David James, © Touchstone Pictures. All rights reserved.; p50 (3) photography by Anne Fishbein, courtesy of the Writers Guild Foundation.

Visual material contributed by Jim Sheridan: p60 (1, 2), with thanks and acknowledgement to Universal Pictures/Hell's Kitchen Films; p61 (3), with thanks and acknowledgement to Universal Pictures/Hell's Kitchen Films.

Visual material contributed by William Goldman: p65 portrait shot; p70 (4), with thanks and acknowledgement to Viking Penguin Inc.

Visual material contributed by Jean-Claude Carrière: p77 portrait shot.

Visual material contributed by Kaneto Shindo: p91 portrait shot; p92 (1), with thanks and acknowledgement to Kindai Eiga Kyokai/Mingei; p95 (11), with thanks and acknowledgement to Toho/Kindai Eiga Kokai/Tokyo Eiga; p96 (1); p98 (1–4), with thanks and acknowledgement to Kindai Eiga Kyokai; p98 (5).

Visual material contributed by Ruth Prawer Jhabvala: p102 (1), with thanks and acknowledgement to Simon & Schuster, Inc..

Visual material contributed by Merchant Ivory Productions for Ruth Prawer Jhabvala: p100 **Heat and Dust**, photography by Christopher Cormack; p101 portrait shot, photography by James Ivory; p102 (2, 3) photography by Christopher Cormack; p104 (1) photography by Sarah Quill; p104–5 (2–4) photography by Sarah Quill; p106 (1) photography by Sarah Quill; p107 (2, 3); p107 (4) photography by Sarah Quill; p110 (1) photography by Derrick Santini; p110 (2) photography by Karan Kapoor; p110 (3) photography by Arnaud Borrel; p111 (4) photography by Erica Lennard.

Visual material contributed by Andrew Stanton: p112 **A Bug's Life** © Disney Enterprises, Inc./Pixar Animation Studios; p113 portrait shot; p115 (1–6) © Disney Enterprises, Inc./Pixar Animation Studios; p115 (8, 9); p116–7 (1) © Disney Enterprises, Inc./Pixar Animation Studios; p119 (3–20) © Disney Enterprises, Inc./Pixar Animation Studios; p120 (1) © Disney Enterprises, Inc.; p122 (1–4); p124–5 (1) © Disney Enterprises, Inc./Pixar Animation Studios.

Visual material contributed by Krzysztof Piesiewicz: p127 portrait shot, photography by Krzysztof Wojciewski; p130 (2); p136 (1) photography by Piotr Janowski.

Visual material contributed by Robert Towne: p140 (1); p141 (2); p142 (1–4), with thanks and acknowledgement to Paramount Pictures; p148 (3, 4), with thanks and acknowledgement to Columbia Pictures; p151 (10).

Visual material contributed by Suso D'Amico: p154 (1).

Visual material contributed by Atom Egoyan: p165 portrait shot, courtesy of Johnnie Eisen, © Ego Film Arts; p167 (4) © Icon Productions; p168 (1, 2) courtesy of Johnnie Eisen, © Ego Film Arts; p168 (3, 4) © Ego Film Arts; p170 (1) courtesy of Johnnie Eisen, © Ego Film Arts; p172 (1) courtesy of Johnnie Eisen, © Ego Film Arts.

Visual material submitted by authors: p20–1 (1–7), with thanks and acknowledgement to Columbia Pictures; p25 portrait shot of George Axelrod, photography by Felim MacDermott; p26–7 (1–9), with thanks and acknowledgement to Paramount Pictures; p39 portrait shot of Steven Zaillian, photography by Felim MacDermott; p45 (3–8), with thanks and acknowledgement to Universal Pictures/Amblin; p53 portrait shot of Jim Sheridan, photography by Felim MacDermott; p55 (1–8), with thanks and acknowledgement to Rank/Castle-Rock-Turner/Hell's Kitchen Films; p56 (3–9), with thanks and acknowledgement to Rank/Castle-Rock-Turner/Hell's Kitchen Films; p60 (4, 5), with thanks and acknowledgement to Universal Pictures/Hell's Kitchen Films; p61 (6, 7), with thanks and acknowledgement to Universal Pictures/Hell's Kitchen Films; p67 (1, 2), with thanks and acknowledgement to MGM/Buttercup Films; p68–9 (1–8), with thanks and acknowledgement to 20th Century Fox; p73 (4), with thanks and acknowledgement to Warner Bros.; p74 (1–3), with thanks and acknowledgement to Paramount Pictures; p79 (1–6), with thanks and acknowledgement to Greenwich Film Productions; p84 (1, 2), with thanks and acknowledgement to Paris Film; p85 (4–9), with thanks and acknowledgement to Paris Film; p87 (1–6), with thanks and acknowledgement to Argos Films; p94 (1, 2), with thanks and acknowledgement to Toho/Kindai Eiga Kyokai/Tokyo Eiga; p95 (3–8), with thanks and acknowledgement to Toho/Kindai Eiga Kyokai/Tokyo Eiga; p104–5 (5–7), with thanks and acknowledgement to Penguin Publishing; p108 (1–10), with thanks and acknowledgement to Merchant Ivory Productions; p115 (7), with thanks and acknowledgement to Disney Enterprises, Inc./Pixar Animation Studios; p118 (1, 2), with thanks and acknowledgement to Disney Enterprises, Inc./Pixar Animation Studios; p121 (2–4), with thanks and acknowledgement to Disney Enterprises, Inc.; p133 (2–7), with thanks and acknowledgement to Polish TV; p139 portrait shot of Robert Towne, photography by Felim MacDermott; p143 (5–10), with thanks and acknowledgement to Paramount Pictures; p145 (3); p147 (4–7), with thanks and acknowledgement to Paramount Pictures/Francis Ford Coppola; p150 (1–8), with thanks and acknowledgement to Paramount Pictures; p151 (9), with thanks and acknowledgement to Paramount Pictures; p153 portrait shot of Suso D'Amico, photography by Felim MacDermott; p156–7 (1–9), with thanks and acknowledgement to Mayer; p167 (1, 2), with thanks and acknowledgement to Icon Productions; p170 (3, 4) photography by Johnnie Eisen, © ego Film Arts; p171 (7, 8), with thanks and acknowledgement to Ego Film Arts.

Remaining visual material: p41 (5) photography by Bonnie Waitzkin, with thanks and acknowledgement to The Random House Group; p59 (1, 2) photography by William L. Rukeyser, © William L. Rukeyser; p92 (5) photography by Haley, © Rex Features; p129 (1) 'The Taking of Christ' by Michelangelo Caravaggio (1571–1610), on indefinite loan to the National Gallery of Ireland from the Jesuit Community, Leeson St, Dublin, who acknowledge the generosity of the Late Dr. Marie Lea-Wilson; p129 (2, 3) photography by Günther Schwarberg, © Günther Schwarberg; p132 (1) photography by Tomasz Korzeniowski; p141 (3–6) photography by John Waggaman, © John Waggaman; p145 (2) portrait of Robert Emmett, with thanks and acknowledgement to the National Museum of Ireland; p168 (5, 6) photography by Patrick Redmond, with thanks and acknowledgement to Blue Angel Films/Parallel Film Productions; p172 (3) photography by Eammon McCabe, with thanks and acknowledgement to Judy Daish Associates Ltd.

index

screenwriting